CIVIL RIGHTS

FOR BEGINNERS ®

CIVIL RIGHTS
FOR BEGINNERS®

PAUL VON BLUM

ILLUSTRATIONS BY
FRANK REYNOSO

FOR BEGINNERS®

For Beginners LLC
155 Main Street, Suite 211
Danbury, CT 06810 USA
www.forbeginnersbooks.com

A For Beginners® Documentary Comic Book
Copyright © 2016

Cataloging-in-Publication information is available from the Library of
Congress.

ISBN # 978-1-934389-89-8 Trade

Manufactured in the United States of America

For Beginners® and Beginners Documentary Comic Books® are published
by For Beginners LLC.

First Edition

10 9 8 7 6 5 4 3 2 1

contents

Illustration by Liz Von Notias

FOREWORD

BY PENIEL E. JOSEPH

The Civil Right Movement represents the most important social and political freedom movement in American history. Its origins date back to the period of antebellum slavery, when enslaved African found themselves in a world that considered them more a species of property than flesh and blood human beings with full citizenship rights.

African American political activism during the period of racial slavery challenged the framework of American democracy culminating in a Civil War (1861–1865) that abolished slavery and ushered in a new era of constitutional citizenship and (male) voting rights. The era of Reconstruction (1865–1877) witnessed an unprecedented flowering of black political and social organizing. African Americans joined political and social clubs, set up schools and churches, and ran for political office on a scale that would have been unimagined only several years before.

The march toward racial equality was halted, then reversed, by the brutal politics of white supremacy which used violence, racist laws, and legislative tricks to inaugurate a system of racial segregation, or Jim Crow, that continues to persist, in some form, until the present day.

The modern civil rights movement, as this book illuminates, has its origins in resistance to slavery and white supremacy by African Americans. Blacks, by virtue of their status on the bottom of America's economic and racial rung, have always been at the cutting edge of radical movements for democracy and racial, economic, and gender justice.

Anti-lynching activist Ida B. Wells innovated a style of black feminism and civil rights advocacy that made her one of the most important social justice figures of the late nineteenth and early twentieth centuries. William Edward Burghardt Du Bois, a Fisk University and Harvard University trained historian, sociologist, and intellectual omnivore, became the 20th century's racial justice avatar through civil rights activism that mixed prodigious scholarship with practical organizing skill that led to the founding of the NAACP in 1909.

The Great Migration of blacks from South to North and the onset of World War I in the early twentieth century helped to reshape the contours of civil rights activism. The landscape of black politics found itself reimagined by Caribbean radicals such as Hubert H. Harrison and the global ambition of the Jamaican Marcus Mosiah Garvey.

Black political activism operated, simultaneously, on several interrelated tracks. The NAACP challenged racial segregation in courts and through its literary publication, *The Crisis,* amassing a steady number of interracial allies in the process. Black nationalists and Pan-Africanists, personified by Garvey's Universal Negro Improvement Association, upheld self-determination as the key to black liberation and promptly started black businesses, political associations, and newspapers whose influence would spread across several continents. Migration transformed urban America, turning cities such as New York, St. Louis, and Chicago into cultural meccas for black artistic, musical, and literary production.

World War II provided space for black political radicals to link the black freedom struggle to the fight against fascism. The "Double V" campaign against the twin evils of Jim Crow and fascism drew figures such as Paul Robeson, A. Phillip Randolph, and Du Bois into robust political alliances. Scarred by the lessons of World War I, when returning black soldiers faced violence and segregation from an ungrateful nation, blacks turned the Second World War into a litmus test for the very concept of democracy and citizenship.

The March on Washington Movement, organized by Randolph and civil rights activists, successfully pushed President Franklin D. Roosevelt into signing an executive order desegregating the military and setting up fair employment practices at the federal level.

Yet despite some victories in labor activism and securing black access to New Deal programs, blacks found themselves largely shut out of postwar American prosperity. The Cold War, which attacked anti-racism as Communist propaganda, made the struggle for social justice more difficult in the 1950s.

The modern Black Power Movement emerged out of this complicated political space. While mainstream media lauded the 27-year-old Martin Luther King, Jr., who emerged as a spokesman for the Montgomery, Alabama, bus boycott in 1956, black New York stood enthralled by Malcolm X, the 31-year-old ex-convict and son of a Garveyite preacher.

Malcolm and Martin came for different branches of the same historical family tree. King, sensing the nation's antagonism to black equality on political grounds (even after the Supreme Court desegregation decision in *Brown v. Board of Education*) initially couched his pleas for justice on moral grounds. Malcolm confronted democracy's jagged edges more bluntly. He blasted white supremacy as a political ideology that had bankrupted the nation's ability to treat blacks as citizens. Malcolm identified American democracy as nothing more than "hypocrisy."

The years between 1954 and 1965 represent the Civil Rights Movement's *heroic period*, an era in which legal and legislative victories (the *Brown* decision, 1964 Civil Rights Act, and 1965 Voting Rights Act); grassroots organizing (the 1955–1956 Montgomery Bus Boycott, 1960 sit-in movement, and 1961 Freedom Rides); massive political demonstrations (the 1963 March On Washington, the 1965 Selma-to-Montgomery demonstration); and political assassinations (Emmett Till in 1955, Medgar Evers and four black girls in Birmingham, Alabama, in 1963, Schwerner, Chaney, and Goodman in 1964, and Malcolm X in 1965) combined watershed political changes with human drama that played out before a national and global audience.

But this period, and the era that followed, can rightfully be considered the time of radical black liberation in America and globally. Malcolm X helped turn the Nation of Islam (a descendant of Garvey's UNIA to which Malcolm's father Earl Little belonged) into a national organization that made inroads with black political radicals. Malcolm found inspiration in 1955's Afro-Asian Conference in Bandung, Indonesia, and 1959's Cuban Revolution. Malcolm met with Fidel Castro in Harlem in 1960 and helped to inspire young SNCC (Student Non-Violent Coordinating Committee) activists and the Black Panthers.

Stokely Carmichael, a young SNCC organizer who knew both Martin and Malcolm, fused these two traditions together during a civil rights march in Mississippi on June 16, 1966. Fresh from an illegal arrest, Carmichael told the crowd of 600 that they now needed to call for "Black Power!" The phrase struck journalists as something new and foreboding, but as Professor Von Blum illustrates in this book, Black Power was part of a much longer tradition of radical civil rights and human rights activism.

That longer tradition, although innovated and founded by blacks, has included a multicultural, multiracial, and multi-generational cast of characters and features a landscape that is global in scope. The black freedom struggle has informed the depth and breadth of what we think of as civil rights, encapsulating movements for women's equality, the environment, LGBT, the physically and mentally challenged, children and the elderly, and indigenous people's rights. It is, without question, the story of the single most important social movement in modern history and one that we must share with each generation.

PENIEL E. JOSEPH is the Barbara Jordan Chair in Ethics and Political Values at the LBJ School of Public Policy and Professor of History at the University of Texas-Austin. He is the author of the award winning *Waiting 'Til the Midnight Hour: A Narrative History of Black Power in America*; *Dark Days, Bright Nights: From Black Power to Barack Obama*; and *Stokely: A Life*. He is an alumnae Caperton Fellow at Harvard University's Hutchins Center and a frequent national commentator on issues of race, democracy, and civil rights.

Chapter 1:

THE HISTORICAL ORIGINS OF THE MODERN CIVIL RIGHTS MOVEMENT

"No human history is rootless, and we see the fullest meaning of the post–1945 events only as we dig deeper. Such probing work could take us back to the coast of Africa, to the earliest liberation struggles on the prison slave ships, and could open up the long, unbroken history of black resistance . . ."

Vincent Harding, We The People: The Long Journey Toward A More Perfect Union in EYES ON THE PRIZE CIVIL RIGHTS READER, 1991

Virtually all Americans and billions of people throughout the world know something about the American civil rights movement, often correctly viewing it as one of the most important political and moral crusades of the 20th century. The movement has entered even the most conventional U.S. history texts and is widely celebrated throughout educational, media, and political institutions in America and elsewhere. In the United States, the major highlights and figures of the civil rights movement are celebrated during African American History Month each February, with television specials, school pageants, public lectures and speeches, governmental resolutions, and a wide variety of special events throughout the nation.

Over the years, moreover, a vast civil rights literature has been created, much of it focusing on the dramatic events of African American resistance to oppression and segregation from the mid-1950s to the early 1970s. Some of this material, however, is scholarly and only marginally accessible to the general public. Moreover, many of the more accessible works focus predominately or even exclusively on this narrow historical timeframe and on widely recognized public figures like Rosa Parks and Dr. Martin Luther King, Jr.

Rosa Parks

Martin Luther King Jr.

Parks and King are iconic figures whose courage and international fame are well earned and entirely justified. But both of these majestic figures would be among the first to proclaim that they stood on the shoulders of thousands who came before them—including countless anonymous women, men, and children who put their bodies, and sometimes their lives, on the line to free their people from slavery, Jim Crow, and more subtle forms of racism. A deeper, more comprehensive history of the civil rights struggles should equally include the lesser-known stories of black liberation struggles and incorporate the efforts of the ordinary people without whom such leaders as Dr. King and others would never have emerged.

The history of the civil rights movement has a continuing vitality in the early 21st century. Its focus on racism still affecting the African American community constitutes an intrinsic feature of a broader vision of modern civil rights history. Its profound impact on other liberation movements it helped to catalyze, including the Chicano Movement, the Asian American Movement, the American Indian Movement, the Women's Movement, and the Gay Liberation Movement, is likewise a crucial part of that history. And the expressive cultural expressions emerging from the political struggles, including powerful developments in literature, music, visual art, and film, also deserve serious attention as part of a broader history of the civil rights movement in America.

The Black Holocaust, from the start of the European slave trade before 1500 to the 19th century, killed millions of African human beings and was a human tragedy of colossal magnitude. Even today, this grotesque historical reality often remains underreported beyond simplistic notions of "the slave trade." Many Americans, including high school and university students, learn about Portuguese, British, French, Spanish, Dutch, and American slave traders who captured Africans of both genders and all ages and treated them as mere cargo, to be transported to the New World as cheaply and efficiently as possible. They also learn that these millions of people were treated barbarously and held as mere property, to be used and abused as labor in developing capitalist societies.

Less well known is the story of resistance in Africa. Many natives, understandably determined to avoid capture, torture, and enslavement, fought their oppressors as soon as the "trade" in human beings began. Many Africans on shore attacked slavers' ships while those already in captivity sometimes revolted against their captors, including at such infamous locales as the Goree Island Slave House (in contemporary Senegal). Even after being driven in chains and with whips from their African homelands, many captured people overcame major difficulties and organized revolts on the slave ships to the Americas. Slavers and their crews responded with larger forces, heavier and more lethal weapons, and even greater brutality and terror.

The 1839 revolt on the Spanish slave ship *Amistad* is probably the most famous example. Sengbe Pieh, known later as Joseph Cinque, led his fellow 53 African captives being transported from Havana against their captors. After gaining control of the ship and armed with machetes, the rebels killed the captain and the cook and ordered the ship returned to Africa. The U.S. Navy captured the *Amistad* and jailed the African rebels in New Haven, Connecticut, charging them with murder. Abolitionists in the United States rose to their defense, and former President John Quincy Adams defended them in court. The black rebels eventually prevailed and the following year returned to Africa.

Joseph Cinque

Steven Spielberg's 1997 film *Amistad* dramatized the events, allowing this early slave ship rebellion to enter American popular culture.

All these resistance activities represent the early origins of the modern civil rights movement. In the truest sense, the civil rights movement began the moment the first Africans resisted the attempt at their capture and enslavement. A fuller glimpse into slave rebellions, in fact, is a valuable foundation for a deeper understanding of the spirit of resistance that motivated the hundreds of thousands of people, predominately but not exclusively African American, who took to the streets, commercial establishments, legislative bodies, and courts of America and finally brought a reluctant nation to an understanding of its brutal, racist past. That understanding must also extend to its continuing legacy into the present.

SLAVE REVOLTS

Human beings crave freedom. Despite the thoroughly racist view that slavery delivered African natives from barbarism to Christian "civilization," the involuntary immigrants who were forced to labor long hours and were regularly beaten and sold as chattel property hated the oppressive conditions into which they have been forced. Thousands of slaves engaged in small individual acts of resistance that provided modest emotional relief and solace in the absence of structural change in their conditions. They worked more slowly in fields and houses than their masters wished; they damaged tools and engaged in minor acts of sabotage; they met secretly and practiced their African religions and spoke their African languages; they produced arts and crafts that indicated their zeal for liberty; and they spoke among themselves of their contempt for their white oppressors in much the same way that their descendants in the South during the 1930s, 1940s, and 1950s spoke disparagingly about their white overseers and employers even while maintaining a surface servility in their presence. All of that reflects the underlying attitudes that formed the roots of the modern civil rights movement of the late 1950s onward.

5

In addition, opposition to slavery took the form of individual and group escapes from bondage to freedom in the North or to Canada. From single departures to organized mass escapes through the Underground Railroad, these activities also reflected the resistance spirit that has always motivated African American freedom struggles.

Iconic figures including Frederick Douglass and Harriet Tubman, after they themselves fled from bondage, became major leaders in the abolitionist movement that played such a major role in the ultimate ending of America's most shameful historical chapter.

Frederick Douglass

Yet the leading expression of black resistance to oppression in the United States was organized slave rebellions, and those efforts should be viewed as the chief early antecedents of later 19th century and 20th century civil rights activities. American slavery was always characterized by violence, mostly by white masters against their captives. This intolerable arrangement generated fierce opposition, often resulting in counter-violence directed against the oppressors.

Historians have documented slave rebellions for many decades. A classic 1943 work by radical historian Herbert Aptheker, *American Negro Slave Revolts*, documented approximately 250 slave revolts from the 1600s to the end of the Civil War. Other historians dispute his figures, asserting that some were minor incidents that were swiftly suppressed. The ultimate number and the specific gravity of the rebellions, however, are far less significant than the underlying spirit of resistance that the slaves revealed in captivity. Aptheker's work was a major catalyst for scholars seeking to understand history from the vantage point of the oppressed rather than from that of the oppressors.

Harriet Tubman

MANY FREE AFRICANS TRIED TO RESIST THEIR CAPTORS, BUT MILLIONS OF MEN, WOMEN, AND CHILDREN WERE CAPTURED AND SENT TO BE ENSLAVED IN THE NEW WORLD.

TO BE SOLD

THERE WERE MANY PEOPLE WHO LED SUCCESSFUL SLAVE REBELLIONS ABOARD SLAVE SHIPS AND IN THE UNITED STATES...

ONE OF THE MOST WELL KNOWN WAS NAT TURNER

Illustration by Liz Von Notias

The most widely recounted slave revolts in U.S. history are the Denmark Vesey uprising in Charleston, South Carolina, in 1822 and the Nat Turner rebellion in Southampton County, Virginia, in 1831. Vesey was a free black man who despised the institution of slavery, with all its attendant cruelty and viciousness. He incited an insurrection, calling on slaves to rise up and liberate the city. Two slaves betrayed Vesey and his confederates, leaking the plot to authorities. Vesey was arrested along with numerous others. In the end, he was convicted and hanged along with 34 others.

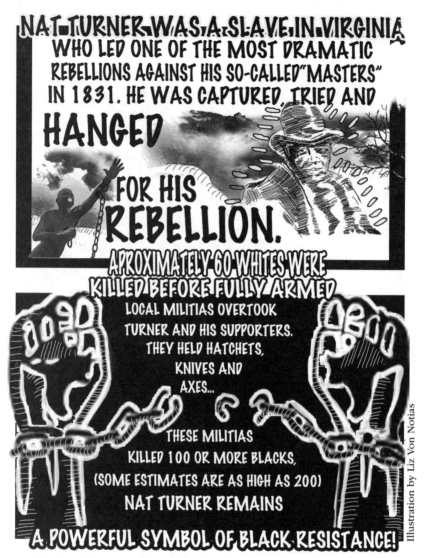

NAT TURNER WAS A SLAVE IN VIRGINIA WHO LED ONE OF THE MOST DRAMATIC REBELLIONS AGAINST HIS SO-CALLED "MASTERS" IN 1831. HE WAS CAPTURED, TRIED AND **HANGED** FOR HIS **REBELLION.**

APROXIMATELY 60 WHITES WERE KILLED BEFORE FULLY ARMED LOCAL MILITIAS OVERTOOK TURNER AND HIS SUPPORTERS. THEY HELD HATCHETS, KNIVES AND AXES...

THESE MILITIAS KILLED 100 OR MORE BLACKS, (SOME ESTIMATES ARE AS HIGH AS 200) NAT TURNER REMAINS A POWERFUL SYMBOL OF BLACK RESISTANCE!

Illustration by Liz Von Notias

Nat Turner, a deeply religious opponent of slavery, organized his rebellion after receiving what he believed was a divine signal. Following his apocalyptic vision, Turner began his mission by gathering supporters, who went from house to house in August 1831, killing the whites they encountered during the insurrection. Approximately 60 whites were killed before heavily armed white militias defeated Turner and his supporters, who had been equipped with knives, hatchets, axes, and blunt instruments. The militiamen killed 100 or more blacks, and another 56 of the insurgents were captured and executed. Violence against blacks continued well after the rebellion had been defeated. Turner avoided capture until October 30 and, after his arrest, was swiftly tried, sentenced to death, and hanged on November 11, 1831.

Nat Turner

In the aftermath of the Turner rebellion, Virginia passed restrictive laws making it even more difficult for slaves to practice religion or to learn to read. Upon execution, Nat Turner became a legendary if controversial figure in U.S. history. In many segments of the African American community, his legacy is regarded as heroic, reflecting the actions of a man who refused to submit to illegitimate power. He is widely regarded as a symbol of militant resistance, a vision that has permeated American civil rights activities since the inception of the American colonies.

Lesser-known slave revolts began long before the formal declaration of U.S. independence in 1776. An early example was the New York slave revolt of 1712, in which several black captives set fire to a building in the city. When white colonists attempted to put out the blaze, the rebels attacked them with guns, hatchets, and knives, killing nine and wounding several others. Twenty-seven slaves were condemned to death in court, and twenty-one were actually executed. Among these were several who were burned alive and one who was broken on the wheel, an especially barbaric punishment involving bludgeoning to death that originated in Europe during the Middle Ages.

A revolt in Louisiana in 1811, also known as the German Coast Uprising, is a key example of a major rebellion that is typically overlooked in conventional U.S. historical narratives. A small army of enslaved men, upwards of 200 or more participants who spoke different languages and who lived on different plantations, mounted a revolt on January 8, 1811, after many months of secret planning. They marched from sugar plantations on the German Coast (located on the east banks of the Mississippi River) toward New Orleans, collecting more men as they progressed. Along the way they burned plantation houses and crops and, armed only with hand tools, killed two white planters while sparing women and children.

But they failed in the dream of establishing a black republic on the shores of the Mississippi River. As ever, white landowners had superior firepower, and territorial officials formed militias to hunt, kill, and capture the black rebels. The results were familiar and brutal: forty-four slaves were tried, convicted, and executed for their role in the uprising. In an especially grisly aftermath, some of their heads were put on spikes and displayed at plantations, presumably to deter other slaves from any form of disobedience.

All of these rebellions, however underreported or insufficiently appreciated, are vital links in the broader origins of modern civil rights activities. Above all, these rebellion showed that African Americans were active participants in the process of liberating themselves—not mere passive observers waiting for a superior or supernatural force to bring them freedom and justice.

THE ABOLITIONIST MOVEMENT

In 1964, at the height of the modern civil rights movement, historian Howard Zinn wrote a book about the Student Nonviolent Coordinating Committee that he titled *SNCC: The New Abolitionists*. Zinn understood intimately the close links between the modern movement and its abolitionist predecessors. The abolitionists and their movements are richly represented in historical and media accounts. The crusade against slavery was never a unified, organized movement and encompassed an extremely large array of organizations with different ideologies and individuals of different races and personalities from the 18th century to the Civil War. From religious groups like the Quakers to political antislavery groups to major African

American figures like Frederick Douglass, Sojourner Truth, David Walker, and Harriet Tubman, these disparate groups and individuals helped end the horrific institution of slavery through their cumulative efforts over decades.

The specific actions and attitudes of black abolitionists and their white colleagues and supporters strengthened the foundation established by slave revolts. A key element was the militant vision of these people—a vision that pervaded anti-racist protests throughout the 19th and 20th centuries and that had a profound resonance in the modern civil rights movement, as Professor Zinn revealed in his book. David Walker, an aggressive black abolitionist, for example, published *Walker's Appeal to the Colored Citizens of the World* in 1829, which advocated black unity and inspired such others as Frederick Douglass to continue the struggle. This radical publication called for slaves to revolt against their masters and was uncompromising in its tone and content. Walker's spirit and passion continued on with subsequent African American resistance figures like W.E.B. Du Bois, Martin Luther King, Malcolm X, and many others.

Escaped slave Frederick Douglass, of course, is one of the iconic Americans of the 19th century. His life, political activities, and oratorical, journalistic, and literary accomplishments have been comprehensively treated, and most Americans have at least a modest acquaintance with his stature and significance. His 1845 autobiography, *Narrative of the Life of Frederick Douglass,* is a compelling view of slavery's barbarism and the spirit of resistance that pervaded Douglass's life and work. Of the many features of this remarkable book, Douglass's encounter as a teenager with Edward Covey, a "slavebreaker," is especially revealing. After numerous beatings by Covey, the young Douglass fought back, eventually prevailing. The result was that Covey never assaulted him again.

Douglass transformed his vigorous

resistance against individual brutality, with its enduring implications for personal dignity and worth, into an entire career of fighting for the oppressed. The same perspective permeated the modern civil rights movements, including Black Power efforts that insisted on the legitimate right of African Americans to self-defense. His abolitionist efforts, encompassing that deeper vision, make Frederick Douglass one of the major figures of African American civil rights history.

Harriet Tubman, too, belongs in that select category, reinforcing the historic contributions of black women to the liberation of their people. Like her abolitionist colleague and ally Douglass, Tubman is also well represented in traditional historical accounts in the United States. A former slave who endured savage beatings as a child, she escaped in 1849 and subsequently became a "conductor" on the Underground Railroad. Most dramatically (and effectively), Tubman returned to the South 19 times or more to lead slaves from bondage to freedom, often across the border to Canada. During the Civil War, she served as a spy, scout, and nurse, augmenting her record as a fierce resistance fighter for people of African descent. Her legacy inspired thousands in the 20th century and beyond to join the continuing efforts for freedom and justice.

No broader historical account of American civil rights activities would be complete without notice of John Brown. Still highly controversial more than a century and a half after his execution, Brown was a radical white abolitionist who advocated and practiced violence in his relentless opposition to slavery. Following his 1859 raid on a federal armory in Harpers Ferry, West Virginia, Brown was captured, tried, and hanged.

Motivated by a powerful religious and moral zeal, Brown and his followers stopped at nothing, including killing pro-slavery supporters, to advance his cause. Though denounced as a terrorist (even now), John Brown helped catalyze the Civil War and exposed the deep national divisions on slavery. The popular ballad "John Brown's Body," sung by Paul Robeson, Pete Seeger, and many others to the melody of "The Battle Hymn of the Republic," helped establish Brown as a martyr whose life was one of the seeds of the modern civil rights movement. His actions also demonstrated that the African American cause occupied the attention of people of all races; white agitators like William Lloyd Garrison and many others were in the fray for many decades. This multiracial reality has permeated the struggle since its inception.

John Brown

The entire abolitionist movement—like all social protest movements—required massive support from women and men whose names and lives will forever be hidden from the history books. These people raised money, sponsored and attended antislavery meetings, distributed and read books, pamphlets, and newspapers, and provided logistical, material, and moral support to slaves fleeing their captivity. For these people, the abolitionist cause was a major focus of their lives. These "ordinary" individuals devoted much of their lives, sometimes at tremendous cost and risk, to the cause of racial justice. Without their individual and collective work, progress would have been seriously retarded. Their efforts provided the deeper substance of the movement; any focus on leaders alone fundamentally misses the essential component of mass political struggle.

POST–CIVIL WAR ERA TO THE 20TH CENTURY

The end of the Civil War brought formal legal rights for blacks in the United States. The primary post–Civil War legal developments were the 13th, 14th, and 15th Amendments to the U.S. Constitution. The 13th Amendment eliminated slavery, the 14th provided for "equal protection of the laws" and other rights made applicable to the states, and the 15th guaranteed full voting rights to black men, including freed slaves. Still, many white Southerners refused to accept the new reality of the end of slavery and legal equality for former slaves. In relatively short time, they commenced effective legal, political, and violent strategies to ensure that political and economic rights would not be realized in actual practice.

The relatively small gains during Reconstruction gave way to horrific anti-black repression, including lynchings, the rise of the Ku Klux Klan in 1868, and the economic system known as sharecropping. This horrific scheme replicated slavery's major advantages to the privileged white population while ironically denying blacks even the marginal security of food and shelter they had enjoyed previously. Among the most egregious measures were the legal barriers to equality. Southern states enacted Black Codes, which restricted black people in numerous ways, primarily to ensure that newly freed blacks would retain the servitude they had experienced under slavery.

The courts were active participants in the institutional drive to preserve white privilege and power after the Civil War. After Congress passed the Civil Rights Act of 1875, which prohibited racial discrimination in public accommodations such as inns, theaters, and places of amusement, the U.S. Supreme Court invalidated the legislation, holding that Congress lacked the power to regulate *private* discriminatory acts. This decision reinforced and promoted the intense racism of the post–Civil War South. It set the stage for subsequent legal decisions that heightened the gaps between black and white citizens and that eroded the equal protection of the law mandated by the 14th Amendment. Like all retrograde actions, however, it also generated a spirit of resistance among African Americans throughout the nation.

As early as 1869, the National Convention of Colored Men of America met in Washington, D.C., to promote suffrage for black men and education for former slaves—goals that remain incomplete well into the 21st century. The National Equal Rights League likewise organized to fight for black rights after the Civil War. African Americans very early on understood the power of collective strength in the protracted battle for legal equality and human rights in the United States.

This organized resistance took a toll. In Philadelphia, Octavius Catto, a young civil rights advocate who rose to a leadership role in the Pennsylvania Equal Rights League, fought vigorously for dignity and equality for his people. Highly educated and eloquent, Catto worked to recruit black troops during the Civil War and supported efforts to desegregate Philadelphia's transportation system and racial

Octavius Catto

segregation in the emerging sport of baseball. His militancy and use of civil disobedience tactics offended many whites in Philadelphia. After passage of the 15th Amendment, Catto labored to persuade black men to vote Republican, and the party pledged to protect America's largest minority population. On Election Day, 1871, black voters faced intimidation from whites, especially Irish Democrats. Catto was assassinated on his way to the polling station, becoming an early martyr for the cause of civil rights. His funeral attracted a large turnout, signifying the broad support of the African American community that has been a constant throughout U.S. history. Not surprisingly, the name of Octavius Catto receives scant mention in contemporary accounts of civil rights history.

By the 1890s, Booker T. Washington emerged as a major figure in African American affairs. A complex man with an ambiguous legacy, Washington promoted a message well outside the militant stream of civil rights movements. The founder of Tuskegee Institute (later Tuskegee University) in Alabama in 1881, he advocated industrial education for African Americans as part of his fundamental accommodationist vision that blacks should adjust to the dominant social and political realities of the times: white supremacy. An astute political operative, Washington attracted substantial white support by advising prominent political and economic leaders and securing financial contributions from major philanthropists. He also attracted support from many African American clergymen and businessmen who appreciated his commitment to avoid confrontation with the powerful white majority.

Despite significant criticism from more militant African Americans, especially in W.E.B. Du Bois's *The Souls of Black Folk* in 1903, Washington helped his people despite his essentially

Booker T. Washington

conservative, nonconfrontational position. He helped to promote the career of renowned black painter Henry Ossawa Tanner and secretly funded litigation for civil rights cases. His educational efforts, though far from ideal, nevertheless advanced opportunities for African Americans in this area. Although few modern civil rights participants understandably view Booker T. Washington with great favor (and many view him with disdain), his historical role can scarcely be ignored.

The 1890s were crucial in catalyzing the powerful civil rights activities of the early 20th century. Another key figure was Ida B. Wells-Barnett, one of many women who have undertaken colossal responsibility in American civil rights activities over the years. Born a slave in 1862, she emerged as a passionate activist as a young woman. A crusading journalist and editor who achieved national and international recognition, she was also a fervent advocate of women's rights throughout her career.

Ida B. Wells-Barnett

Like many African Americans who turned to political action, Wells-Barnett encountered racism through dramatic first-hand experience. In 1884, she refused to abandon her train seat when a conductor ordered her to move to an uncomfortable segregated car on a journey from Memphis to Nashville. This action (71 years before Rosa Parks's heroic refusal in Montgomery, Alabama) led her to file suit against the railroad. She initially prevailed, but lost on appeal in the Jim Crow legal system of the late 19th century South.

Another incident with close personal linkages was the primary catalyst for Wells-Barnett's most famous civil rights efforts. A lynch mob in 1892 murdered three of her friends in Memphis; this was a grotesque act that propelled the young Wells into a lifetime of anti-lynching activism. In response, she published a pamphlet titled *Southern Horrors: Lynch Law in*

All Its Phases, and A Red Record that documented the murderous violence against African Americans and revealed how the perpetrators used allegations of rape against white women as an excuse for their criminal acts. The same outrageous lie continued to justify lynchings of black men for the next half century in the South.

Wells traveled through the United States and Europe on behalf of her crusade, raising awareness of an issue that would be on the front burner of the civil rights agenda for decades to come. After her marriage to Chicago lawyer Ferdinand Barnett, she became editor of a black newspaper called *The Conservator*. Even after the birth of her children, she continued her civil rights activism, organizing for women's suffrage and covering racial issues as a journalist. Her death in 1931 ended a life of profound commitment to racial and gender justice, marking Ida B. Wells-Barnett as one of the major influences on those who followed the path of turning black discontent into morally based, effective social action.

The 1890s, however, added additional burdens on the African American population. The evaporation of legal rights for blacks extended to the Supreme Court's support of state laws that sanctioned racial discrimination. The notorious case of *Plessy v. Ferguson* in 1896 institutionalized segregation for the next six decades, ensuring second-class citizenship for millions of African Americans. Homer Plessy, a mixed-race man who was seven-eighths white and one-eighth black, looked white and, in the language of the era, could have "passed." He was arrested and jailed in 1892 after taking a seat in the white car and refusing to remove himself to one reserved for persons of the "colored race." His defiance of the Louisiana segregation law requiring blacks to sit in separate railroad cars was part of a deliberate challenge organized by the Citizens Committee, a multiracial group established in New Orleans in 1891.

Homer Plessy

The group was composed of black professionals who used the courts to challenge laws that promoted racism and maintained blacks in inferior political, social, and economic positions. In its document titled "An Appeal," they made their objectives clear:

"No further time should be lost. We should make a definite effort to resist legally the operation of the Separate Car Act. This obnoxious measure is the concern of all our citizens who are opposed to caste legislation and its consequent injustices and crimes...

We therefore appeal to the citizens of New Orleans, of Louisiana, and of the whole union to give their moral sanction and financial aid in our endeavors to have that oppressive law annulled by the courts.

We call for such a demonstration as will plainly show the temper of the people against that infamous contrivance known as the 'Jim Crow Car'..."

Although the Committee and Homer Plessy lost the legal fight when the Supreme Court validated the infamous doctrine of "separate but equal," the effort reflected a key feature of the overall struggle for racial equality in the United States. Many decades later, African American legal figures including Charles Houston, Thurgood Marshall, and Constance Baker Motley would reaffirm that legal strategy, this time with more favorable results.

John Hope

Although the U.S. Supreme Court (with only one courageous dissenting opinion by Justice John Harlan) dashed the hopes of Plessy, the Citizens Committee, and millions of blacks throughout the South, the infamous decision became a stimulus for additional protest. One especially powerful voice came in 1896 from John Hope, who became prominent educator and civil rights leader in the early 20th century. Hope revealed the kind of sterling oratory that has characterized civil rights activity in America in a Nashville address in 1896:

"Rise, Brothers! Come let us possess this land. Never say 'Let well enough alone.'. . . Be discontented. Be dissatisfied. . . . Be restless as the tempestuous billows on the boundless sea. . . ."

PLESSY v. FERGUSON

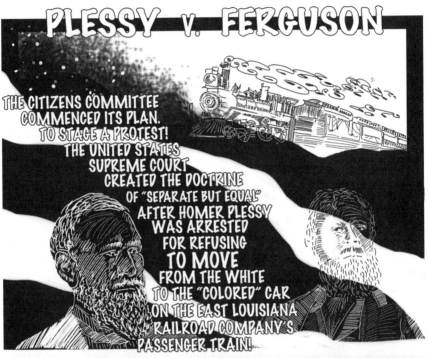

THE CITIZENS COMMITTEE COMMENCED ITS PLAN, TO STAGE A PROTEST! THE UNITED STATES SUPREME COURT CREATED THE DOCTRINE OF "SEPARATE BUT EQUAL" AFTER HOMER PLESSY WAS ARRESTED FOR REFUSING TO MOVE FROM THE WHITE TO THE "COLORED" CAR ON THE EAST LOUISIANA RAILROAD COMPANY'S PASSENGER TRAIN!

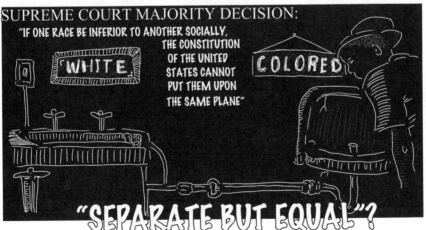

SUPREME COURT MAJORITY DECISION:

"IF ONE RACE BE INFERIOR TO ANOTHER SOCIALLY, THE CONSTITUTION OF THE UNITED STATES CANNOT PUT THEM UPON THE SAME PLANE"

WHITE

COLORED

"SEPARATE BUT EQUAL"?

That spirit would emerge strongly in the dawn of the new century. Its force would remain unabated for more than fifty years and plant the seeds of resistance that would shake America to its very foundations.

Chapter 2

MODERN STIRRINGS: THE EARLY 20ᵀᴴ CENTURY THROUGH THE 1940S

BEGINNINGS

From the turn of the 20th century to the present day, African Americans and their allies have mounted persistent and effective resistance to pervasive racism. Black people and their leaders and spokespersons, living under legal discrimination, grinding poverty, and daily threats of violence began to mobilize to counteract these conditions and compel mainstream America to live up to the ideals it promulgated in its founding documents and post–Civil War constitutional amendments.

John Hope's spirit of resistance was deeply felt throughout the African American community, even when few opportunities were present for effective political action to counteract the destructive consequence of white racism validated by the 1896 *Plessy* decision. Still, early 20th century organizational stirrings began to set the stage for the vigorous activities of a half-century later. The emerging figure of Dr. W.E.B. Du Bois, who played such a giant role in his people's struggles for racial dignity and social and economic justice, catalyzed one of the most significant developments in 1905. His book of two years before, *The Souls of Black Folk*, had specifically repudiated Booker T. Washington's strategy of gradualism and advocated a militant agitational response to American racism. He communicated with sixty prominent African American professionals, seeking to mobilize a leadership group to pursue a black freedom agenda.

W.E.B. Du Bois

William Trotter

John Hope

Frederick Mcghee

With William M. Trotter, John Hope, Frederick McGhee, and several others, these men met on the Canadian side of Niagara Falls and vigorously critiqued Booker T. Washington's policy of accommodation. The organization became known as the Niagara Movement, which organized committees, created state chapters, distributed publications, and commenced a program of protest against the extant Jim Crow arrangements that dominated much of American life. Its initial Declaration of Principles reflected the militant vision that would infuse black political action for the remainder of the century. The following provisions, written principally by Du Bois, reflected the tone and spirit of the entire movement:

Protest: We refuse to allow the impression that the Negro-American assents to inferiority, is submissive under oppression and apologetic before insults. . . .

Oppression: We repudiate the monstrous doctrine that the oppressor should be the sole authority as to the rights of the oppressed. The Negro in America is stolen, ravished and degraded, struggling up through difficulties and oppression. . . .

Agitation: Of the above grievances we do not hesitate to complain, and to complain loudly and instantly. To ignore, overlook, or apologize for these wrongs is to prove ourselves unworthy of freedom. Persistent manly agitation is the way to liberty, and toward this goal the Niagara Movement has started and asks the cooperation of all men of all races.

The emphasis marked a dramatic rhetorical departure from a cooperative relationship with white power. The movement also demanded justice in the legal system, suffrage for women, and equity in housing, the military, employment, and education. At its second conference in Harpers Ferry, West Virginia, in 1906, the Niagara Movement reiterated its militant demands and paid homage to such abolitionist leaders as John Brown, Nat Turner, William Lloyd Garrison, and Frederick Douglass, reinforcing the historical continuity of the civil rights struggle in America.

Lasting four years and disbanding as a result of funding and organizational problems, the Niagara Movement was a forerunner to the National Association for the Advancement of Colored People (NAACP), formed in 1909 by a diverse group of whites and African Americans including Du Bois and Ida B. Wells-Barnett. A key catalyst for the creation of the NAACP was white violence directed against black people. A tragic incident in 1908 in Abraham Lincoln's hometown of Springfield, Illinois led to the burning of black-owned businesses and death so both black and white citizens, a pattern that would soon be repeated in other locations with even

Ida Wells-Barnett

W.E.B. Du Bois

greater costs in life and property. Another catalyst was the horrific record of lynching in America, which continued despite the courageous efforts of Ida B. Wells-Barnett and others.

Du Bois was initially the sole African American to serve in a staff role in the new civil rights organization. He became the founding editor of the NAACP's journal *The Crisis*, where his influential editorials and other writings had an enduring impact on the civil rights movement for many decades. Although the NAACP had a less radical agenda than its Niagara Movement processor, it focused its efforts on the pervasive (and growing) racism in the nation, including the laws that fortified segregation in the South and elsewhere.

An early NAACP action involved its mass protests against the 1915 silent film *The Birth of a Nation*, D.W. Griffith's racist "classic" that glorified the Ku Klux Klan and that portrayed African Americans in egregiously stereotypical roles as childlike buffoons and as male sexual predators lusting after virginal white women. White men in blackface played these sexually uncontrollable black men, signifying the racism of the era and adding further insult to the nation's African American residents. President Woodrow Wilson, a staunch segregationist himself, arranged a viewing of the film at the White House and is reported to have praised it highly.

The NAACP organized its members nationally to boycott the film and protest its offensive depictions. Marches occurred throughout the United States, and some African Americans picketed movie theaters and even engaged in civil disobedience. Some cities refused to permit its showing as a result of these protests. The most enduring result of the efforts against *The Birth of a Nation* involved the growing power of mass black action, a precursor of the events that soon became a hallmark of American domestic social and political life.

D.W. Griffith

Another major focus of the organization's early civil rights activities was its role in the protracted legal struggle against U.S. racial discrimination— probably the most well-known feature of the NAACP in its long and distinguished history. From its inception, the organization sought to implement the legal guarantees of the U.S. Constitution, and specifically the rights guaranteed in the 13th, 14th, and 15th Amendments added in the aftermath of the Civil War. An early victory occurred in 1915, when the U.S. Supreme Court found the grandfather clause exemptions to literacy tests unconstitutional in *Guinn v. United States*. The NAACP targeted this exemption as an outrageous mechanism, though just one of many, to deprive African Americans of their 15th Amendment right to vote.

James Weldon Johnson

The selection of noted lawyer, writer, diplomat, and scholar James Weldon Johnson as field secretary of the NAACP in 1916 marked a significant advance for the organization. Johnson helped increase the NAACP's membership from 9000 almost tenfold, while augmenting the role of local chapters. He became one of the major public faces of the NAACP and intensified its political and legal efforts. The NAACP spent considerable effort fighting the scourge of lynching, which was central to the civil rights agenda in the early 20th century. Its New York office, for example, displayed a black flag with the words "A Man Was Lynched Yesterday" to inform the public about each incident.

Johnson and Du Bois also encouraged the use of mass demonstrations, which later became the emblem of modern civil rights activism. The silent protest of 10,000 African Americans in New York City on July 28, 1917 to protest lynching and the murder, injuries, and property destruction against black residents of East St. Louis, Illinois, earlier that month was the first major civil rights demonstration of the 20th century and one of the most dramatic actions in U.S. history. The marchers were ordinary African American women, men, and children from all walks of life. They were the backbone of black protest and resistance, without whom no progress or advances were possible then or in subsequent decades.

The growth and development of the NAACP coincided with many other civil rights developments at the time. One of the most significant was the establishment of the Universal Negro Improvement Association (UNIA) under the leadership of Marcus Garvey. Founded originally in Jamaica in 1914, UNIA moved to Harlem, New York, in 1916. Unlike W.E.B. Du Bois, who saw the problems of black people as essentially political, with political solutions, Garvey's perspective was primarily economic, cultural, and psychological, making himself and Du Bois longtime rivals in American civil rights activist history.

Marcus Garvey

UNIA sought to energize black people by generating pride in Africa and African ancestry. In the 1920s, it recruited more than a million adherents. Garvey believed in an eventual return to the African motherland. He created a movement replete with symbols and ceremonies; its parades through Harlem and other African American centers drew thousands of participants and spectators. UNIA developed various business enterprises to support the cause, including an international passenger and commercial shipping line called Black Star Lines. UNIA was the most popular expression of Pan-Africanism at the time. Above all, Garvey's movement instilled pride in the working-class masses of Harlem and elsewhere, providing a vision of racial dignity and solidarity that endured throughout the civil rights movement and that grew even more intense during the Black Power movement that emerged in the late 1960s.

Many African American veterans of World War I found UNIA's message especially compelling. More than 350,000 blacks served honorably in that conflict, in segregated units where they were usually relegated to support roles and prevented from seeing combat. They believed that their service should entitle them to equal treatment and racial justice upon their return. They assumed that America would reward their efforts to help "make the world safe for democracy" by implementing genuine democracy at home.

They were profoundly mistaken. Throughout the country between May and October 1919, shortly after the end of the war, white riots against African Americans occurred in dozens of cities. These riots followed the demobilization of military personnel and reflected widespread white fears about unemployment and historical patterns of racial scapegoating. Many African Americans, including returning veterans, responded with armed resistance—continuing the tradition of militant rebellion from Nat Turner and others during the days of slavery.

James Weldon Johnson called the riots the "Red Summer," a label that has endured as a description of a disgraceful era of American racial history.

Johnson organized protests against the carnage, augmenting the NAACP record of peaceful civil rights action. W.E.B. Du Bois likewise urged his fellow African Americans to resist, lamenting the shame of American racism. In *The Crisis*, he wrote: "We return *from* fighting. We return *fighting*."

Many black veterans found Marcus Garvey's message emotionally liberating, and they became a major component of the UNIA organization. But Garvey's movement was flawed in numerous ways, including his lack of a concerted political vision; Du Bois was a major rival and Garvey had powerful enemies in the African American community. Du Bois had written, accurately, that Garvey was a stubborn and domineering leader, with bombastic methods that caused needless animosity among African Americans. He also criticized UNIA for its cozy relationship with white supremacists. Garvey, meanwhile, became personally vulnerable to governmental persecution. He was sentenced to federal prison on questionable charges of mail fraud in 1925 and deported two years later to Jamaica. In the long term, however, his contributions to the civil rights struggle are both unquestionable and enduring, especially his profound belief in black dignity and the linkages of persons of African heritage to their African roots.

THE 1920S THROUGH THE 1940S

The early 1920s saw a frightening and despicable increase in violence against African Americans. The riots in East St. Louis were scarcely the only egregious example of white carnage and destruction. In 1921, numerous black residents were killed in Tulsa, Oklahoma, where a vibrant, affluent black community was burned to the ground. Thousands of African Americans were incarcerated and left homeless. In 1923 in Florida, a state with a high number of lynchings, a white mob destroyed the black town of Rosewood, causing substantial loss of life and property damage. Such racial violence, of course, only increased African American resistance, a phenomenon that has been a constant factor of civil rights activity since slavery.

Various other developments in African American life also influenced the growing commitment to organized civil rights activities. In 1925, A. Philip Randolph organized and became the president of the Brotherhood of Sleeping Car Porters, the first African American labor union in the United States. Randolph had earlier involved himself in socialist organizing and editorial work for the magazine *Messenger*, developing a commitment to collective action that would serve as the foundation for his union and civil rights efforts for decades to come. As a union head, he helped African American railroad porters, who had been seriously exploited and underpaid by the Pullman Company, gain better wages, overtime pay, and shorter hours, making them among the most respected workers in the African American community.

In subsequent years, Randolph played a huge role in the civil rights movement. Although the labor movement and the civil rights movement occasionally clashed, they were more regularly allies in a broader commitment to human rights that included

A. Philip Randolph

BROTHERHOOD of SLEEPING CAR PORTERS

Train, Chair Car, Coach Porters and Attendants
AN INTERNATIONAL UNION
Affiliated with the A. F. of L.

both worker and racial justice. Most significantly, they shared a common commitment that included mass demonstrations, sit-ins, picketing, boycotts, and other tactics designed to exert maximum pressure on their adversaries.

Another major union that combined both labor and civil rights concerns was the Southern Tenants Farmers Union (STFU), organized in 1934. The STFU was open to both black and white sharecroppers, among the poorest and the most exploited American workers. It realized that an integrated organization was both principled and pragmatic, although in some Southern locations it still had dual locals. The STFU identified strongly with the Baptist Church and the Socialist Party. It engaged in militant actions to protect its members from plantation owners and the violent thugs they employed against the union. Local police forces working at the behest of the growers, often acting with brutal violence, were also regularly deployed against the STFU. In December 1934, a delegation from the SFTU occupied the office of Secretary of Agriculture Henry Wallace, an early sit-in of the kind that became ubiquitous three decades later in in the South and elsewhere. The union regularly quoted scripture in its meetings and rallies and sang "We Shall Not Be Moved," later one of the major anthems of the civil rights movement.

One of the most powerful and durable features of the American civil rights movement has been its strategy of seeking redress against racism and discrimination in the courts. This strategy began systematically in the early part of the 20th century, largely under the aegis of the NAACP. The chief initial figure associated with the legal drive toward civil rights was Charles Houston, an African American graduate of Harvard Law School. Houston provided the leadership and vision that has endured throughout the organization's entire history.

Charles
Huston

Charles Houston joined the law faculty at Howard University in 1924 and eventually helped build it into the premier law school for black students. He served as the functional head of the institution, which created a tradition of training lawyers to lead the fight against racial injustice. In 1935, he was appointed Special Counsel to the NAACP. Under his guidance, the NAACP developed a strategy to "chip away" at the pernicious impact of *Plessy v. Ferguson*. Among many other actions, Houston played a major role in Marian Anderson's historic 1939 Easter concert at the Lincoln Memorial in Washington, D.C., after the Daughters of the American Revolution barred her from its Constitution Hall venue because she was black. Houston was involved in a majority of NAACP-sponsored civil rights cases until his death, after which his Howard Law School student, Thurgood Marshall, continued his record of legal triumphs, including cases that fundamentally challenged and reversed the historical pattern of American racism.

One of the most dramatic legal battles occurred in 1931, when nine teenage boys were falsely accused of rape in Scottsboro, Alabama. This charge, which regularly led to the lynchings of black males, reflected the pervasive white view of black men's predatory sexual impulses against white women, the same defamatory view expressed earlier in *Birth of a Nation*. In three trials, all the boys were convicted by all-white juries and each, except for 13-year-old Roy Wright, was sentenced to death—the usual sentence for black defendants convicted of raping white females and what most African Americans and their supporters regarded as nothing but a legal lynching.

On appeal, the case continued for several years, with both the NAACP and the Communist Party USA providing legal assistance, occasionally clashing over strategy and ideology. Their differences aside, both groups agreed that the case was a major example of judicial injustice based on race. It evoked national and even international attention, galvanizing sympathy for the growing black movement. While some of the Scottsboro defendants served substantial time in prison, none was executed and the case itself catalyzed even more civil rights activity on all fronts, including legal actions directed against the same racist system that perpetrated the Scottsboro abomination.

The Great Depression of the 1930s caused misery to most Americans, including blacks, who suffered enormously from the declining employment opportunities in addition to the burdens of discrimination. African Americans increased their protest activities during this era by organizing marches, picket lines, and labor actions with integrated unions. At the heart of their civil rights efforts were employment issues, which became a highly visible focus of the movement in the late 1950s and 1960s. During the Depression, African American picketers and some white supporters marched in front of businesses in black neighborhoods that maintained racially exclusive hiring policies. In some cities, picket signs that read "Don't Buy Where You Can't Work" dominated the protests; the same slogan proved ubiquitous several decades later. The civil rights efforts of the 1930s had some impact, forcing white business owners to begin employing African American workers. Equally important, the protests began generating a sense of militancy among black people and leaders alike, generating a sense of hopefulness about racial progress and justice.

Dorothy
Height

Ella
Baker

Anna Arnold
Hedgeman

In New York, the appalling working conditions of African American women also generated aggressive resistance actions that have remained largely underreported in many civil rights histories. The Young Women's Christian Association (YWCA) was the organizational base of several black women activists who fought tenaciously against the exploitation of black domestic workers. Anna Arnold Hedgeman, Ella Baker, and Dorothy Height, all of whom became iconic figures in the modern civil rights era decades later, mobilized forces and public opinion to protest these conditions. Among their targets was the infamous "Bronx Slave Market," where wealthy white housewives picked up black women on a daily basis to clean their houses and do their laundry. Wages were low, treatment was degrading, and the black women regularly suffered debilitating injuries and other physical disabilities from their labors. Ella Baker co-authored a stunning exposé of the Bronx Slave Market in a 1935 issue of *The Crisis*.

A. Philip Randolph

Franklin D. Roosevelt

The start of the 1940s continued the unbroken history of black resistance and came to establish an important chapter in American civil rights history. A dramatic challenge to the administration of President Franklin D. Roosevelt set the tone for several protest and legal actions throughout the decade. Roosevelt and many members of his administration had been sympathetic to the African American community, but they had taken little practical action to combat segregation, lynching, and other expressions of American racism.

A. Philip Randolph was distressed in early 1941 at the lack of job opportunities in the defense industry as the United States was gearing up for probable war. In May, he issued a "Call to Negro America to March on Washington for Jobs and Equal Participation in National Defense on July 1." Union members from the Brotherhood of Sleeping Car Porters spread the word throughout the country, helping to organize March on Washington committees and rallies.

The March on Washington Movement generated extensive grassroots efforts in black communities throughout the nation. Once again, it was intended to involve ordinary people whose lives and incomes were directly affected by discrimination. President Roosevelt tried to persuade Randolph to call off the march, making an appeal for national unity in the face of the impending Nazi threat. Randolph refused, threatening to assemble as many as 100,000 marchers. Roosevelt capitulated and issued Executive Order 8802, banning discrimination in defense industries and establishing the Fair Employment Practices Committee. Randolph then called off the march and showed that mass action—or the threat of mass action—could accomplish significant, concrete objectives in the continuing drive for racial equality.

Protests against racial injustice continued in other arenas as well in the early 1940s. In New York, Adam Clayton Powell, Jr., pastor of Harlem's enormous Abyssinian Baptist Church, organized picket lines for jobs in white-owned stores in the neighborhood. Even earlier, he had organized picket lines in front of the Empire State Building, the headquarters of the 1939 New York World's Fair, to demand that officials hire more blacks for the event. His Sunday sermons were calls to social action, and he mobilized parishioners to become active political players in the struggle for equal employment opportunities. Powell, later a Congressman with a career-long civil rights agenda, used the power of the black church, historically combining religion, spirituality, and social organizing and political action. Like many black pastors over the decades, Adam Clayton Powell moved easily from the pulpit to the street as part of a broader commitment to social and racial justice.

James Farmer

Chicago was also a major locus of early 1940s civil rights activism. Several Christian activists, including James Farmer and Bayard Rustin, who later became giant figures of the 1960s civil rights movement, were members of the Fellowship of Reconciliation, a pacifist

38

organization influenced by Mohandas Gandhi. In 1942, they and several others founded the Congress of Racial Equality (CORE), which began a series of aggressive local actions against racial discrimination. CORE targeted restaurants, theaters, amusement parks, and other public accommodations that practiced segregation. An initial action was directed against the Jack Spratt Coffee House on Chicago's South Side, which had been blatantly hostile to African American customers. After months of fruitless negotiations, escalating tactics, finally culminating in occupation of the entire establishment, resulted in success. These became the foundation for the organization's strategies and tactics during the height of 1960s civil rights efforts in both the South and North.

By 1947, CORE had grown to a national campaign. On April 9, sixteen men, equally divided between black and white, boarded buses in Washington, D.C., on a "journey of reconciliation" to the South. Refusing to accept the segregated seating arrangements of the era, they were physically assaulted and several were arrested and jailed. This became the model for the freedom rides of 1961 that propelled the modern civil rights movement into international prominence.

Civil rights organizations also vigorously promoted the success of highly visible African Americans who entered fields that had historically excluded them. The most dramatic example of the 1940s was the celebrated appearance of Jackie Robinson as a member of the Brooklyn Dodgers in 1947, making him the first black player in modern major league baseball. Robinson's pioneering effort and his personal courage in the face of despicable racial invective (and worse) during his initial season are well known and properly acknowledged.

Jackie Robinson

Paul Robeson

Still, Jackie Robinson's ascension to baseball history and stardom actually resulted from ongoing efforts to integrate the major leagues. As early as 1943, Paul Robeson had led a delegation of eight black publishers to the office of Baseball Commissioner Kennesaw Mountain Landis, to meet with the owners of the sixteen major league teams. Robeson spoke passionately, drawing on his own experiences of racism as a star athlete at Rutgers University and his great celebrity as an actor, singer, civil rights activist, and public intellectual. He assured the owners that integration would proceed smoothly and that it was "the best in the American spirit."

Protracted political pressure from Robeson and other luminaries played a vital role in eroding the resistance to change professional baseball. Some leftist unions demonstrated for an end to segregation in the sport, and the black and communist presses pressed for an end to baseball's racial barriers. Wendell Smith of the *Pittsburgh Courier* and Sam Lacy of the *Baltimore Afro-American* regularly reported on efforts to integrate the major leagues.

Another key figure was Lester Rodney, longtime editor of the communist *Daily Worker*. He wrote repeatedly about African American athletes and called the exclusion of blacks from major league baseball "un-American" and "the crime of the big leagues." For all its flaws, the Communist Party, including its call for equality and justice in sports, was usually an outstanding ally of the forces for civil rights throughout the 20th century. The prominence of Jackie Robinson, heroic in itself (but still largely symbolic), reflected a deeper principle of civil rights efforts throughout American history: change results from political struggle, not from the moral epiphanies from those with power and privilege.

Lester Rodney

BATTLES IN THE COURTS

Concurrently, the NAACP continued to pursue its strategy of legal action to combat racial discrimination. In 1931, Walter White became executive secretary of the organization and intensified its legal efforts. In 1936, Charles Houston's former student at Howard, Thurgood Marshall, left his private law practice and began his lengthy legal service for the NAACP. His personal background reflects the civil rights zeal he brought to his advocacy and to his later career as a federal appellate judge and the first black U.S. Supreme Court justice. After graduating from historically black Lincoln University, Marshall was unable to enroll in the University of Maryland Law School

Thurgood Marshall

because it barred African American applicants. Later, as a lawyer, he successfully sued to end its exclusionary policy.

Working with Houston, Marshall won a number of landmark cases that changed the legal landscape on race in the United States. He and his contemporary and later legal colleagues, including Jack Greenberg, Constance Baker Motley, Robert L. Carter, William Hastie, Derrick Bell, Harold Boulware, Spottswood Robinson, Loren Miller, and others showed immense personal courage in traveling to the South to investigate claims and initiate litigation. Although they encountered segregated facilities and considerable racial hostility, the unsung plaintiffs were equally courageous, remaining in the South to face even more sustained hostility from racist whites and their institutions.

One of Thurgood Marshall's initial legal triumphs was to begin reversing the systematic denial of voting rights against African Americans and other minorities. He attacked the "white primary," a mechanism first established by internal political party regulations and subsequently by state law. Throughout the South, the Democratic Party had dominated the political system, with winners of the party primary elections routinely winning the general elections. In 1944, Marshall and his legal colleagues challenged a 1935 U.S. Supreme Court ruling that held that the Democratic Party was a private organization that could determine its own membership and qualifications.

An 8–1 Supreme Court ruling in the case of *Smith v. Allwright* overturned its earlier decision, holding that the plaintiff, African American Lonnie Smith, was essentially disenfranchised when he was excluded from voting in the Texas Democratic Party primary. The majority opinion explicitly stated that the Democratic primary was held under state statutory authority and that the U.S. Constitution grants *all* citizens a right to participate in elections. The Court was clear in stating that the white primary was merely a mechanism to deny blacks their constitutional right to vote.

The legal component of the civil rights movement continued aggressively when Marshall supported with an *amicus curiae* brief the 5000 Mexican American students in Orange County, California, who sued to end the discrimination they faced in public schools based on their ethnicity. In 1947, in the case of *Westminster School District v. Mendez,* the U.S. Court of Appeals for the Ninth Circuit became the first federal appellate court to hold that school segregation violates the 14th Amendment. Houston's strategy of chipping away at legal segregation had received another major boost.

The NAACP and Thurgood Marshall shifted their relentless legal assault on segregation by focusing on housing in the post–World War II period. Housing discrimination had a long and dishonorable history in the United States. A chief mechanism to enforce it was the restrictive covenant, a legal obligation in a deed that requires the buyer to perform (or not perform) some activity or obligation. In 1948, Thurgood Marshall and Loren Miller won the landmark case of *Shelly v. Kraemer*, in which the Supreme Court held that state enforcement of racially restrictive covenants that bar African Americans from buying houses in white neighborhoods

Robert R. Carter

Spottswood William Robinson III

Constance Baker Motley

Thurgood Marshall

Charles Houston

43

violates the 14th Amendment. The Court reasoned that enforcement of the covenants constitutes state action and is therefore applicable to Constitutional prohibition under the equal protection clause of that amendment.

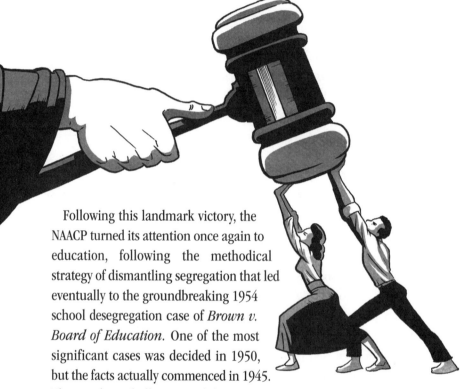

Following this landmark victory, the NAACP turned its attention once again to education, following the methodical strategy of dismantling segregation that led eventually to the groundbreaking 1954 school desegregation case of *Brown v. Board of Education.* One of the most significant cases was decided in 1950, but the facts actually commenced in 1945. Thurgood Marshall presented the case against a bogus "separate but equal" law school in Texas and pursued the case all the way to the U.S. Supreme Court.

Heman Sweatt, an African American postal clerk, wanted to become a lawyer. As a Texas resident, he applied to the University of Texas Law School at Austin, the premier law school in the state. Denied on racial grounds, Sweatt sued in state court to compel his admission. But the state court refused. Instead, it gave the state six months to supply substantially equal facilities for black law students. It was apparent to Marshall

Heman
Marion
Sweatt

and everyone else that this was patently absurd; no decent law school could be created so swiftly. Texas responded by offering a sham program with a few faculty members, few books, and no accreditation. The trial court judge nevertheless ruled that the new law school was substantially "equal" and therefore in compliance with the standards of *Plessy v. Ferguson.*

The U.S. Supreme Court reversed this ludicrous judgment, clearing the way for *Plessy's* ultimate demise. The opinion revealed the hypocrisy and deceit of the entire "separate but equal" standard. Heman Sweatt entered law school at the University of Texas, but a combination of emotional exhaustion and physical problems caused him to abandon his studies. He eventually completed a master's degree in social work at Atlanta University and worked for many years with the Urban League. But like Thurgood Marshall, he was a major and heroic figure in the early 20th struggle for civil rights; unlike Marshall, he never gained comparable visibility. Without unsung individuals like Heman Sweatts, the long trajectory of civil rights struggles could never have succeeded.

As America entered the second half of the 20th century, it was clear to everyone, but especially to citizens of African descent, that the times indeed were changing. The dawn of a new decade, with its optimism and postwar prosperity, would propel the civil rights movement into a new phase—a phase that would lead inexorably to the explosions of the 1960s and beyond.

EMMETT TILL

(1941-1955)

AT HIS FUNERAL IN CHICAGO, EMMETT'S MOTHER MAMIE TILL, PLACED HIS BEATEN AND MANGLED BODY IN AN OPEN CASKET SO THAT THE WORLD WOULD SEE THE HORROR OF HIS RACIST MURDER!

Illustration by Liz Von Notias

Chapter 3

THE 1950S: BEGINNINGS OF THE MODERN CIVIL RIGHTS MOVEMENT

THE CHIEF CATALYSTS: EMMETT TILL AND *BROWN V. BOARD OF EDUCATION*

Historians and laypersons alike perceive the decade of the 1950s as the beginning of the modern American civil rights movement. The famous Montgomery bus boycott and the emergence of such iconic figures as Rosa Parks and Dr. Martin Luther King, Jr. have commanded the major (and sometimes exclusive) attention of media and educational accounts. Unquestionably, the dramatic events in Montgomery stirred the nation's conscience and propelled the civil rights movement into a major new phase. But the Montgomery story is much more layered than many people realize, and the other racial events of the 1950s, some well-known and some lesser known, are inextricably linked to the broader history of American civil rights.

Two events preceding the Montgomery conflict are widely and properly viewed as the chief catalysts of the modern civil rights movement. The first was the culmination of the NAACP legal strategy to break the grip of racial segregation once and for all. Thurgood Marshall was the lead counsel when he brought the *Brown* case to end school segregation nationally. It was not clear what the result would be when he first initiated the litigation. The ascendancy of Earl Warren to the position of chief justice of the Supreme Court, however, made a huge difference. Warren brought strong political skills to the office as a former California governor, state attorney general, and county district attorney. He was able to persuade his judicial colleagues to vote unanimously for the plaintiffs in *Brown v. Board of Education,* which helped establish Warren as one of the most progressive justices of the Court in the modern era.

The *Brown* decision is one of the landmark cases in U.S. constitutional history; it has spawned a large literature and in some ways assumed a mythic character beyond its actual significance in integrating public schools in the South and elsewhere. Still, Chief Justice Warren's words on May 17, 1954 had a powerful psychological influence on African Americans generally and on the burgeoning civil rights movement that would soon change the course of American history: "We conclude that in the field of public education the doctrine of 'separate but equal' has no place. Separate educational facilities are inherently unequal."

Judge Earl Warren

The decision prompted strong responses, both favorable and unfavorable, throughout the nation. African Americans were generally pleased that the Supreme Court had finally recognized their legal rights and human dignity. A dramatic example of the profound emotional impact is found in the reaction of Robert Williams, then a young African American serving in the U.S. Marine Corps:

"My inner emotions must have been approximate to the Negro slaves' when they first heard about the Emancipation Proclamation. Elation took hold of me so strongly that I found it very difficult to refrain from yielding to an urge of jubilation. . . .On the momentous night of May 17, 1954, I felt that at last the government was willing to assert itself on behalf of first-class citizenship, even for Negroes. I experienced a sense of loyalty that I never felt before. I was sure that this was the beginning of a new era of American democracy."

—Robert Williams,
Can Negroes Afford To Be Pacifists?,
New Left Review, Jan./Feb. 1960

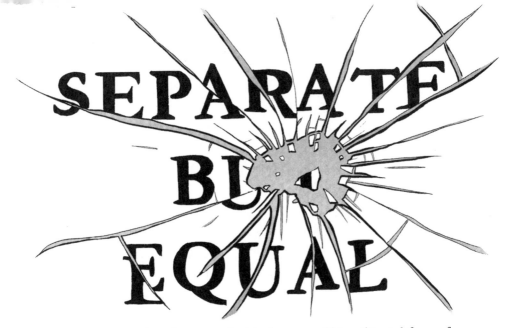

SEPARATE BUT EQUAL

Williams, who later became a fugitive because of his militant defense of his people, believed that the *Brown* decision would alter the course of history for African Americans. The decision and reactions like his were partially responsible for energizing the civil rights movement at the time. Many white Southerners saw it differently and began campaigns of massive resistance to preserve the racist social, political, and educational order. Their efforts came to include closing public schools, blatant defiance of federal law, and overt violence against African American children seeking entrance to schools in compliance with the *Brown* ruling. The Supreme Court, indirectly and unintentionally, gave Southern resisters an impetus with its 1955 implementation decision, known as *Brown II*. In it, the justices left it to lower local courts to decide specifically what remedies would be appropriate in effecting the integration order, saying only that it should be implemented "with all deliberate speed." Many Southern officials took the vague language as an excuse to delay any implantation whatsoever. In the end, however, Southern intransigence and defiance only reinforced the will of African Americans to move even more vigorously to bolster their ongoing civil rights efforts.

The second major catalyst of the modern civil rights movement was the tragic murder of 14-year-old Emmett Till in August 1955 in Mississippi. The facts of the case are well known. Till was from Chicago and visiting relatives near Money, Mississippi, when he allegedly whistled at, or spoke "disrespectfully" to, the wife of a white store owner in town. As a Northerner,

Emmett Till

Till knew little or nothing about the deeply engrained racial taboos of the Deep South. A few days later, storeowner Roy Bryant and his brother-in-law, J.W. Milam, drove to the cabin of Till's uncle, Mose Wright, and proceeded to abduct, torture, and murder the boy. Three days later, authorities found Till's grotesquely mutilated body in the Tallahatchie River.

The case generated widespread national publicity. Bryant and Milam were arrested and Till's mother, Mamie Till, held an open-casket funeral in Chicago. *Jet* magazine published a photograph of young Till's mangled face, allowing the nation and the world to see the unspeakable consequences of racist violence in Mississippi.

The trial of Bryant and Milam in Sumner, Mississippi, was a ludicrous display of the racist judicial system that had prevailed since the end of Reconstruction. The courtroom itself was racially segregated; even Michigan Congressman Charles Diggs, who traveled to Mississippi to witness the proceeding, was seated at a card able with black reporters. Mose Wright identified the murderers when he famously pointed at them and said "Dar he" (there he is) in front of the all-white jury, which returned a not-guilty verdict after about an hour of "deliberation." Although Wright's testimony was inevitably fruitless, he revealed the kind of simple human courage that formed the underlying fabric of American civil rights history.

The case had a powerful impact on African American communities and their growing activism. Just as *Brown v. Board of Education* aroused widespread hope, the murder of Emmett Till and the racist exoneration of his killers generated equally widespread rage. The combined responses helped form the foundation of the emerging movement, especially with the increasing truculence of white racist political officials and others throughout the South. The black press went on the offensive in following the Till murder, editorializing for the need for government action and increased black vigilance.

A massive 1955 rally in New York City to protest the Till murder reflected the convergence of the black church, labor, and the traditional civil rights community in a progressive coalition that would prevail throughout the 1960s. Held in an African American church, the rally featured A. Philip Randolph of the Brotherhood of Sleeping Car Porters and the NAACP; other unions and many white supporters were also in attendance. Randolph's powerful oratory highlighted the Till case in defining the broader civil rights agenda, including school desegregation, Southern racism, voting rights, and even the emerging struggle against African colonialism. He noted the courageous efforts of Mamie Till and Mose Wright and urged those in attendance to support the NAACP and to enlist others to do the same.

Mose Wright

This was also the early age of television, and electronic communications spread the news rapidly. White citizens began to realize what African Americans had known for generations: the law was different for blacks and whites, and blacks were no longer willing to accept this and the other injustices of a pervasively racist Southern and national landscape. The injustice of the Till murder case resonated far beyond the African American population.

THE MONTGOMERY BUS BOYCOTT

The civil rights revolution of the mid-20th century began dramatically a little more than a year later. The first battle occurred in Montgomery, Alabama, the "Cradle of the Confederacy," a city where the black population lived mostly under rigid Jim Crow customs and laws. City buses were especially humiliating for the thousands of African American passengers who depended on them for their daily transportation needs.

The system was simple. White riders sat in the front and black riders sat in the back. The middle section was open to blacks unless white riders needed the seats, in which case black passengers were obligated to move further back. If a bus was full, black passengers had to stand, regardless of gender and age. When boarding, black riders frequently paid at the front, left the bus, and boarded again at a separate door in the rear of the vehicle. White bus drivers sometimes compounded the indignity by treating black passengers rudely and leveling racial slurs at them. No one of any race had any illusions about the degrading system; everyone knew that it reflected and reinforced the long-held notion of black inferiority.

Montgomery had a growing cadre of black activists and a few white supporters who were eager to challenge the racist public transportation system. Other challenges had occurred before Montgomery in 1955. In 1944, Jackie Robinson refused to move to the back of a bus while serving in the U.S. Army. Arrested and court-martialed, he was acquitted. In 1953, African Americans organized a brief bus boycott to protest segregation in Baton Rouge, Louisiana. And earlier in 1955 in Montgomery, 15-year-old high school student Claudette Colvin was removed from a public bus and arrested after refusing to give up her seat to a white man.

E.D. Nixon

Civil rights leaders, especially E.D. Nixon, had initially hoped to use the Colvin incident as a test case. She was unwed and pregnant and had screamed when placed in handcuffs. Though not the ideal figure that Rosa Parks shortly became, young Colvin's spirit nevertheless reflected the growing sense of defiance that infused African

Americans, especially the young. In October 1955, 18-year-old Mary Louise Smith, also of Montgomery, likewise refused to vacate her seat for a white passenger. She, too, was arrested for her act of defiance. But Nixon was concerned that Smith's father was an alcoholic and that she lived in a poor clapboard shack, making her a less than exemplary test case figure. Thus, in the end, Mary Louise Smith was another one of the courageous but unsung figures without whom the history of the civil rights movement would be incomplete.

Nixon was a key figure who catalyzed the rebellion that changed and intensified the course of American civil rights history. He was a longtime labor leader who had served as Alabama branch president of A. Phillip Randolph's Brotherhood of Sleeping Car Porters union as well as heading both the state and local NAACP. Nixon was also effective as an unofficial advocate for the African American community, helping Montgomery blacks with various grievances against public officials. With a lifetime of civil rights activism and consciousness, E.D. Nixon wanted to end the degrading system of bus segregation.

Rosa
Parks

In Rosa Parks, he found the perfect person to mount the challenge. Parks, a secretary for the local NAACP, had an abiding commitment to social and racial justice, a calm demeanor, and a personal character beyond reproach.

Despite the romanticized versions of her life and portrayals still common in elementary school lessons and some mass media accounts, she was not a tired, elderly seamstress who simply refused to give up her seat on the bus to a white person. She was an educated woman with a history of activism; she had followed the Scottsboro case and had attended rallies protesting the more recent murder of Emmett Till and other black victims of racial violence; she had participated in a race relations workshop at the progressive and racially integrated Highlander Folk School in Tennessee; and at the time of her historic arrest on Thursday, December 1, 1955, she was only 42 years old.

The events surrounding her arrest were not especially dramatic. Parks left work and boarded her regular bus to go home. She sat in the middle "no-man's land" when the bus driver ordered her and three other African American riders to move to the back. The driver told them to "make it light on [themselves]." Rosa Parks was the only one to refuse his order. The driver notified her that she was under arrest and called the Montgomery police, who transported her to jail and booked and fingerprinted her. Parks telephoned her mother, who contacted E.D. Nixon. He, in turn, contacted liberal white lawyer Clifford Durr, who arranged Parks's release on bail.

Jo Ann Robinson

Nixon recognized the extraordinary impact of the arrest. He pleaded with her to make this a test case to challenge segregation on the Montgomery bus system. Parks decided to cooperate, despite the disapproval of her husband, who understandably worried about her safety. Nixon began organizing immediately, contacting several sympathetic friends, including lawyer Fred Gray, who agreed to represent Parks in court. Gray also contacted Jo Ann Robinson of the Women's Political Council, beginning the movement that would transform U.S. political and social history.

E. D. Nixon

Martin Luther King Jr.

Another major figure in the protracted struggle in Montgomery, Robinson taught at all-black Alabama State College. Parks's arrest mobilized her to spring into action. She and her friends clandestinely mimeographed 35,000 leaflets on the Alabama State campus throughout the night. The leaflets contained strong language about black people's rights and the indisputable fact that the survival of Montgomery's bus system depended on black patrons. It called upon the city's African Americans to stay off the buses the following Monday to protest Parks's arrest and trial. Robinson and the Women's Political Council distributed the leaflets throughout the African American community.

The events that followed have become deeply ingrained in the fabric of modern U.S. history. With the active engagement of E.D. Nixon, Dr. Martin Luther King, Jr. emerged as president of the Montgomery Improvement Association (MIA), which spearheaded the long and ultimately successful bus boycott. Nixon sought King because he was young (26 years old), new to Montgomery, and a powerful public speaker. Throughout the long campaign, King worked closely with his longtime friend and associate, the Reverend Ralph David Abernathy, himself a major leader in the modern civil rights movement.

Martin Luther King revealed early on his majestic powers of oratory and persuasion. His stirring words ("If we are wrong, God Almighty is wrong") marked him as a man both of the moment and of history, and the crowd seemed to know it intuitively. The response, reflecting the energy of the black church, made a systematic protest that inevitably dredged up not only the discourtesies and humiliations on the city's buses, but the deeper centuries of racism and oppression. The time had truly arrived for a mass movement to challenge the foundation of racial injustice. Throughout the protracted struggle in Montgomery, King worked with many colleagues, including Abernathy, Nixon, Robinson, and Bayard Rustin, another iconic figure of American civil rights history.

Jo Ann Robinson

E.D. Nixon

Ralph David Abernathy

Bayard Rustin

After the success of the one-day boycott, Montgomery's African American citizens decided to continue their campaign. Initially, the MIA proposed a modest desegregation compromise, but the bus company and city officials rejected any arrangement that would lead to racial dignity for black riders. Meanwhile, black drivers in the segregated taxi system facilitated the boycott by charging ten cents per ride, the same fare that passengers paid to ride the bus. City officials promptly responded by announcing that they would prosecute any drivers charging less than the 45-cent minimum fare, the first of several actions that the whites in power attempted to use to break the collective actions of the black community.

The essence of the Montgomery bus boycott involved the persistent will of the community and its creative mechanism to stay away from the bus system. Various black churches, for example, organized private taxis and carpools to transport workers to their destinations. Some sympathetic white women used their own vehicles to transport their African American domestic works to and from their houses, often evoking the disapproval of their husbands and neighbors. Above all, black workers, including many middle aged and elderly women, walked to work, sometimes several miles each way. As the boycott continued, these walkers created a powerful sense of community solidarity, underscoring their political will and ensuring the ultimate success of their effort.

Resistance was fierce because white supremacy yielded slowly and unwillingly. Unlike the nonviolent boycotters, white racists had no qualms about improper, even violent tactics. White police officers regularly stopped black carpool drivers and issued citations for trivial or even nonexistent offenses. Jo Ann Robinson was the victim of this police harassment, receiving numerous citations during the boycott.

Dr. King's home was bombed on January 30, 1956, and E.D. Nixon's home was bombed on February 1. Municipal authorities also relied on legal mechanisms, including a 1921 statute prohibiting interference with business. As Dr. King and several other boycott leaders faced arrest and indictment, the world saw in newspaper photographs and on television screens the spectacle of the young civil rights leader convicted and jailed. This national exposure provided major financial and moral support to the Montgomery bus boycott. Throughout the entire time, the boycott brought significant economic damage both to the bus company and to white business interests that depended on black patronage.

On June 5, 1956, a federal district court ruled in *Browder v. Gayle* that Alabama's law requiring racial segregation on buses was unconstitutional. One of the plaintiffs in this case was Claudette Colvin, the teenage girl who was arrested even before Rosa Parks for defying the segregation statute. On December 17, the U.S. Supreme Court rejected city and state appeals and affirmed *Browder v. Gayle*. On December 20, the African American citizens of Montgomery called off their boycott after 381 days of struggle. Dr. King, Reverend Abernathy, and several other African Americans boarded a city bus, signifying the end to the most dramatic and successful mass movement for racial justice in the 20th century.

Decades later, disputes continued to fester among scholars and laypersons alike about the allocation of credit for the Montgomery victory. In his magisterial civil rights history book *Parting the Waters*, for example, Taylor Branch devotes some attention to the question of how much credit should go to Dr. King, E.D. Nixon, Rosa Parks, Jo Ann Robinson, and the Women's Political Council. The debate is fruitless, as there is plenty of credit to go around. In the end, however, no one should overlook the extraordinary contributions of the thousands of ordinary African Americans who refrained from riding the buses for more than a year. Their courage, resilience, good humor, and sheer physical stamina in the face of white anger, harassment, and brutality were nothing short of heroic. Brilliant oratory, organizational effectiveness, compelling leadership, and legal acumen all played an indispensable role in that historic victory, but without the genuine will of the common people, nothing durable would have been accomplished.

The Montgomery bus boycott had implications far beyond the integration of city buses. It catalyzed civil rights activities throughout the South and throughout the entire nation. It propelled Dr. Martin Luther King into a national leadership role, which lasted until his untimely murder in 1968. Above all, it empowered millions of African Americans to understand that they could control the course and direction of their own lives by concerted political action. That recognition would dominate the next decades of domestic political life in the United States.

HOUSING DISCRIMINATION AND RESISTANCE

Lesser-known civil rights activism in the 1950s focused on residential segregation. Although these struggles rarely achieved the same media coverage as the bus boycotts, school desegregation protests, and later sit-in demonstrations and freedom rides, their significance to African American life is real if insufficiently appreciated. Residential locations determine many features of life that are inextricably linked to their quality. Better schools, lower crime rates, access to superior public services, higher-quality shopping centers, and often healthier air quality, among many other factors, are prevalent in some neighborhoods and conspicuously lacking in others, especially those with large concentrations of low-income racial and ethnic minority residents.

Moreover, home ownership is a major mechanism through which Americans have acquired wealth and entered the middle class. African Americans who have been able to purchase homes in previously all-white neighborhoods have been able to take advantage of this arrangement. Far more frequently, African Americans have been confined to ghetto areas through legal restrictions, real estate manipulation, and economic hardship. Even when the U.S. Supreme Court outlawed restrictive covenants in 1948, white residents worked assiduously to restrict their neighborhoods, seeking alliances with realtors and bankers who continued to employ discriminatory practices to restrict African Americans to limited areas in cities and towns. Redlining, a practice that designated and isolated specific minority neighborhoods where lenders refused to extend credit to African American purchasers, was pervasive.

When blacks did buy homes in white neighborhoods, resistance was often fierce and violent. This phenomenon was scarcely confined to the 1950s. In the most celebrated case of the early 20th century, Dr. Ossian Sweet, a black physician, bought a house in 1925 in a previously all-white neighborhood of Detroit. Reaction was swift: a mob gathered and shots were fired. Dr. Sweet or one of his defenders returned fire and killed one of the racists attacking his house. Sweet and his defenders were indicted and tried for murder. In a highly publicized trial, where both the NAACP and famed lawyer Clarence Darrow assisted, most of the defendants were acquitted. Subsequently, the state dropped charges against Dr. Sweet.

In 1954, an equally dramatic housing issue occurred in Shively, a suburb of Louisville, Kentucky. An African American couple, Andrew and Charlotte Wade, wanted to buy a house in an all-white neighborhood, but could not because of racist housing practices. Carl and Anne Braden, a white couple, agreed to purchase the house for the Wades and deed it over to them. The Bradens, both journalists, were leftists, politically active, and deeply committed to civil rights and full integration, an unpopular view in their essentially Southern locale.

After the Wades moved in, their racist neighbors burned a cross on their front yard, broke their windows, and dynamited the house. The Wades and the Bradens came under constant attack for race mixing and for alleged Communist ties. In another egregious example of judicial injustice, Carl and Anne Braden were charged with sedition, under the assumption that working for housing integration was an expression of Communist subversion. Carl Braden was sentenced to 15 years in prison and actually served eight months before being released. The Kentucky sedition law was eventually declared unconstitutional, and all charges were dropped. The Wades moved backed to Louisville, and the Bradens continued their civil rights activism for the rest of their lives. Anne Braden wrote a full account of the ordeal in her 1959 book *The Wall Between*.

Three years later, in Levittown, Pennsylvania, a similar conflict occurred when another African American family purchased a house in a newly created all-white Philadelphia suburb. Levitt & Sons had built the community with affordable houses designed primarily for working- and lower-middle-class white residents seeking to flee crowded cities with increasing minority populations. The company steadfastly refused to sell to African Americans, claiming that their presence would conflict with the attitudes of white residents, most of whom wanted to preserve a white enclave and who worried about their property values.

In 1957, a group of sympathetic whites was determined to break Levittown's color line. Among them were Lew and Bea Wechsler, Peter and Selma Von Blum, and Sam Snipes, who with others found a young African American couple, William and Daisy Myers, who needed a larger house for a growing family. William Myers was a World War II veteran and an ideal homebuyer for the property. The sympathetic whites tried to smooth their path, but a racist grassroots effort to prevent their entry into Levittown began and intensified.

The night the Myerses moved in, hundreds of angry white homeowners rioted outside their house, fueled by racist hatred and alcoholic consumption on a hot August evening. The riots continued for several days and the resistance leaders formed the "Levittown Betterment Committee," which engaged in a series of hostile actions. Members shouted racial slurs, played "Dixie" on loudspeakers, and drove caravans of cars with Confederate flags in front of the Myers's home. Individual insults against the Myerses and their friends were also common, and the entire city was enveloped in a climate of racial hysteria.

The Myers's windows were broken, the Wechslers' home was defaced with the letters "KKK," and the Von Blums' home was the site of a Klan-led cross burning. Allegations of Communist affiliation were regularly made against the Myerses and their supporters. But William and Daisy Myers and their children remained in Levittown, weathering the concerted efforts to force them out and refuting the absurd allegations that property values would decline and that "mongrelization" of the races would inevitably follow.

As historian Thomas Segrue notes, the struggles to integrate Levittown and Shively deserve as prominent a place as Montgomery, Little Rock, Birmingham, and Selma in civil rights history. Affordable and decent housing is crucial to racial justice and dignity, and these battles were vital in the continuing struggle for that result. Equally important, the role of pioneering figures like Andrew and Charlotte Wade and William and Daisy Myers and their fearless supporters reveals yet again the power of ordinary people to alter the course and direction of history.

THE BATTLE OF LITTLE ROCK, 1957

The "Battle of Levittown" attracted national attention for a few months. Jackie Robinson and Paul Robeson, among many other luminaries, followed the events and expressed support for the Myerses and their allies. But developing racial events in Little Rock, Arkansas, soon shifted national and world focus to the continuing Southern resistance against school integration despite the legal mandate under the 1954 *Brown* decision. Many Southern senators, representatives, and other public officials, for example, promoted the "Southern Manifesto," which called on states to oppose school integration despite the Supreme Court order.

Several states enacted laws that delayed school integration. In Virginia, some counties actually closed their public schools rather than allow black children to attend with white children. In Prince Edward County, in fact, schools remained shuttered for five years. These actions remained popular with large numbers of the white population. White Citizens Councils and other racist groups used the *Brown* decision to augment their membership and power. More ominously, they often engaged in economic retaliation and violence against African Americans seeking to implement their rights under the Constitution.

The start of the 1957–1958 school year in Little Rock marked the first major confrontation between a state and the federal government over school integration. Under federal court order, the Little Rock School Board was required to admit black students to all-white Central High School. Daisy Bates, president of the Arkansas branch of the NAACP, recruited nine young women and men to attend Central High. But on the first day of school, an angry white mob gathered in front of the school and Governor Orval Faubus ordered the Arkansas National Guard to prevent the students from entering. NAACP lawyers, including Thurgood Marshall, got a legal order preventing Faubus from blocking the students' entrance.

September 4, 1957 was the first day of the school year—and a day that has come to live in infamy. Daisy Bates's plan was to have all nine students arrive together. But one student, Elizabeth Eckford, had not learned of the plan. She arrived alone and was greeted with curses, racist jeers, and threats to her physical safety—even her life. Eckford quickly abandoned her attempt to enter school and fled in tears to a nearby bus stop. One courageous white woman, civil rights activist Grace Lorch, protected her and guided her to the bus back home.

Orval Faubus

Pandering to white racist sentiment, Governor Faubus warned that "blood will run in the streets" if the federal government interfered. He and President Dwight Eisenhower negotiated over the standoff while the nine students remained blocked from attending class. Mobs continued to protest school integration, using familiar racial invective and threats and actual violence. When the governor removed the National Guard, the students were left with no protection at all

President Eisenhower was forced to respond to the nation's most severe constitutional crisis since the Civil War. He federalized the Arkansas National Guard and ordered federal troops to protect the African American students

Dwight D. Eisenhower

and compel their entry into Central High School. As president, he well understood that he could not permit a state governor to defy the federal courts; he knew that federal law and authority had to prevail and that he had no choice but to act with superior force. But Eisenhower was personally unmoved by any vision of racial justice. Physical and emotional violence against black Americans evoked little passion in him. The successes of the civil rights movement of the late 1950s and early 1960s owe little to the Republican president who reluctantly stood up to Governor Faubus. Eisenhower was well aware that the world was watching and that, in the Cold War atmosphere, he could ill afford to allow the overt racism in Little Rock to dominate national and international news.

The nine students finally gained admittance to Central High on September 25, arriving in Army vehicles with armed guards. Each day, the students had individual guards to escort them to classes, while they faced verbal taunts and physical attacks from white students. A few classmates and the military guards showed sympathy, but most support came from their families, the black community, Daisy Bates, and their own courage. They endured the entire year, living under media scrutiny and without the social lives enjoyed by regular high school students. One of the nine, Minnejean Brown, was expelled for defending herself against repeated attacks. In May, the oldest of the Little Rock nine, Ernest Green, graduated. He was the first African American student to graduate from Central High School. His family and Dr. Martin Luther King attended the ceremony.

The following academic year, Governor Faubus closed Little Rock's public high schools in a further move to avoid integration. In December 1959, the U.S. Supreme Court ruled that the schools had to reopen, paving the way, finally, for African American students to enjoy their legal right to a public education. Faubus's recalcitrance ensured his reelection, but also focused national and world attention on the continuing racial injustices in the United States. More than anything, it further mobilized the emerging civil rights movement, making the dramatic events of the new decade of the 1960s inevitable.

African Americans throughout the South and elsewhere followed the events in Little Rock and other racial upheavals closely. They understood that the old system of segregation and black passivity were coming to an end and that they would be the agents of change. At the same time, more systematic organizing efforts began to develop that would transform the face of race in America even more radically.

Ernest Green

Ella Baker

Fred Shuttlesworth

Bayard Rustin

Ralph Abernathy

Joseph Lowery

Earlier in 1957, after the Montgomery bus boycott, Dr. King invited several African American ministers to meet in Atlanta. There they formed the Southern Christian Leadership Conference (SCLC), which included Bayard Rustin, Rev. Ralph Abernathy, Rev. Fred Shuttlesworth, Rev. Joseph Lowery, and others who became major figures in the modern civil rights movement. Dr. King became president of SCLC, and Ella Baker became its sole staff member. Its focus was on nonviolent mass action and protest as the mechanism to achieve civil rights. This advocacy was controversial because many black church leaders thought that legal action alone should suffice and that direct action would invite white economic and physical retaliation.

Throughout the 1960s, the more militant approach of Dr. King and his colleagues revealed the wisdom of that strategy. By the start of the new decade—the quintessential era of 20th century agitation—the civil rights movement was, quite literally, on the march. America was watching closely.

Chapter 4:

THE 1960S: GOLDEN AGE OF THE CIVIL RIGHTS MOVEMENT

Scholars and the general public regard the 1960s as the major era of the modern nonviolent civil rights movement. The growth of older civil rights organizations and the creation of newer, more militant ones intensified the struggle of African Americans for genuine equality. Tactics like sit-ins and freedom rides were resurrected and highly visible in the television age. Dramatic civil rights confrontations in Albany, Georgia; Birmingham, Alabama; Selma, Alabama, and many other places became the dominant headlines of the day. The historic March on Washington in August 1963, the Mississippi Freedom Summer in 1964, and the tragic murders of civil rights leaders and volunteers in Alabama, Mississippi, and elsewhere also dominated domestic consciousness.

The emergence of national civil rights figures like John Lewis, Stokely Carmichael, James Foreman, James Farmer, Fannie Lou Hamer, and so many others brought African American leadership to major and unprecedented prominence. Historic civil rights legislation like the Civil Rights Act of 1964 and the Voting Rights Act of 1965, born of the massive street protests in the South and throughout the country, added legal muscle to the post–Civil War constitutional amendments that had been long ignored. But above all, the persistence and courage of thousands of ordinary human beings, primarily African Americans but also men, women, and children of all backgrounds and ages who put their bodies and lives at risk made the 1960s one of the most momentous periods of American history. Many of these people were so profoundly committed to the cause of racial justice that they willingly went to jail for their beliefs, often suffering economic hardship and social ostracism.

SIT-IN DEMONSTRATIONS

The civil rights decade of the 1960s began auspiciously on February 1, 1960, when four young students from historically black North Carolina A&T College in Greensboro decided to protest the exclusion of African Americans from a Woolworth's store lunch counter. Joseph McNeil, Franklin McCain,

Ezell Blair, and David Richmond sat down at the counter and politely requested service and were refused. They remained seated until the store closed. This was the same sit-in tactic that had previously been employed in labor and civil rights agitation, but now the action had much wider implications.

In the days that followed, many more North Carolina A&T students, as well as those from nearby all-black women's Bennett College, joined the Woolworth's sit-in. By then, newspaper and television media coverage brought the action to broad public attention. The impact was swift and dramatic. On February 3, more than sixty people came to Woolworth's, and more than three hundred showed up on February 4. The protest spread to Kress, another five-and-dime store in Greensboro. Lunch counter personnel continued to refuse to serve them, white customers expressed hostility, and the sit-in demonstrators remained peaceful and polite.

News of the Greensboro actions spread rapidly throughout the South. Sit-ins commenced in several other North Carolina cities and towns and to other states. One student in Nashville, John Lewis, who had attended workshops on nonviolence conducted by Reverend James Lawson, swiftly joined the emerging sit-in movement in Nashville. This led to the successful desegregation of lunch counters in that Tennessee city. Both Lewis and Lawson become nationally visible leaders in the nonviolent civil rights movement, with stellar moral and political accomplishments throughout the 20th and early 21st centuries.

As the sit-in movement grew, white resistance intensified, especially when the targeted stores began feeling the adverse economic impact of the protests. White customers sometimes attacked sit-in participants physically, beating them with their fists and pouring catsup and other substances on them. Many demonstrators were arrested and white police officers often acted brutally, clubbing the sit-in participants while hauling them off to jail. Except for a few incidents, the protestors adhered to nonviolence and maintained a dignified demeanor that captured the world's attention.

By April 1960, the sit-in movement had become the major focus of the civil rights movement. In Greensboro, Woolworth's capitulated and in July began serving all customers, including African Americans. The movement soon spread to other public accommodations, including transportation, beaches, parks, swimming pools, libraries, and other facilities that continued the racist culture that had prevailed in the South since *Plessy v. Ferguson*. The militant actions of young people, primarily students, began to change the entire character of the civil rights movement.

Ella Baker, executive director of the Southern Christian Leadership Conference, was among the first of the older civil rights activists to understand the significance of the new wave of black uprisings. She organized a conference of Southern student sit-in leaders and Northern activists in Raleigh, North Carolina, to explore the future development and possibilities of the movement. Baker wanted to mobilize the energy of young people into a cohesive political force, drawing on her own extensive experience as an organizer since the 1930s.

Ella Baker

Through her assistance, the Student Nonviolent Coordination Committee (SNCC) was formed. SNCC soon became the leading militant civil rights organization in the South, with an open, more democratic form of governance. Baker resigned her SCLC position and began a long association with SNCC, serving as a mentor to such prominent figures as Julian Bond, Bob Moses, Stokely Carmichael, Bernice Johnson Reagon, and others. Students became the backbone of the mass movements that swept the region, becoming some of the most effective leaders and the foot soldiers of the entire movement.

Stokely Carmichael

Bob Moses

Bernice Johnson Reagon

Julian Bond

The wave of student activism convinced Dr. King to join the sit-in protests. He was arrested in Atlanta in October 1960 and sentenced to jail. This arrest occurred during the final weeks of the close presidential election between Republican Vice President Richard Nixon and Democratic Senator John Kennedy. After extensive political maneuverings, Senator Kennedy placed a sympathy phone call to King's wife, Coretta Scott King, and Kennedy's brother Robert made King's arrest and imprisonment an issue of national attention. Black voters appreciated the Kennedys' concerns, however politically motivated, and turned out in large numbers to help elect the Massachusetts senator to the presidency in November.

FREEDOM RIDES

Despite the sit-ins' substantial successes, much of the South remained as rigidly segregated as ever, despite legal prohibitions against racial practices. James Farmer, head of CORE, announced a plan to resurrect the journey of reconciliation that the organization had pioneered in 1947. This time it targeted the facilities that faced interstate travelers, including waiting rooms, restrooms, and eating establishments in Greyhound and other bus stations below the Mason/Dixon line. And this time the tactic was called the "Freedom Rides," with hundreds of African American and white women and men boarding buses to converge on the segregated bastions.

The first Freedom Ride began on May 4, 1961, when seven black and six whites departed from Washington, D.C. on two buses. They deliberately violated the segregation rules and encountered only mild resistance until entering Alabama. Outside the town of Anniston, racists, including KKK members, burned one bus and attack the riders. In Birmingham, a white mob, with the active complicity of local police led by Commissioner Eugene "Bull" Connor, attacked the freedom riders with fists, pipes, chains, and bats, causing severe injuries to some of the riders.

The violence embarrassed the new Kennedy Administration, which, reflecting its caution on civil rights matters, urged restraint. But the key civil rights groups, including CORE, SNCC, and SCLC, all agreed that the Freedom Rides had to continue in the face of violent white resistance. SNCC leaders John Lewis and Diane Nash were especially adamant on this point.

On May 20, a freedom bus left Birmingham bound for Montgomery. Alabama state troopers accompanied the bus, but left at the Montgomery city line. When the riders arrived at the bus station, white racists, men and women alike, met them again with clubs, pipes, and other weapons. Shouting racist slurs, they beat the riders mercilessly, with no Montgomery police in sight. A U.S. Justice Department official, John Seigenthaler, was knocked unconscious, while John Lewis was seriously injured. In March 2013, Montgomery police chief Kevin Murphy formally apologized to Lewis, by then a longtime U.S. Congressman, for the appalling lack of police protection more than a half century before.

John Lewis

Two more buses with freedom riders left Montgomery on May 29 bound for Jackson, Mississippi. Accompanied by highway patrolmen and the National Guard, they arrived in Jackson without incident. Immediately afterwards, however, Mississippi officials arrested them for breach of the peace. Loaded into police wagons, they were booked into local jails and, after these facilities filled up, transferred to the notorious state penitentiary in Parchman.

Conditions there were brutal and the civil rights prisoners were treated harshly, with no air conditioning, lack of sheets and mattresses, and abusive language from guards, among other hardships. Approximately three hundred freedom riders were incarcerated at Parchman, including many college and university students. On September 22, 1961, the U.S. Interstate Commerce Commission issued an order banning segregated facilities in bus and train stations. But the larger victory was the impact of the sit-ins and freedom rides on national consciousness: America had seen the brutality of racism and the courage of those who dared opposed it, especially the young African Americans and others who gave up their ordinary lives for a greater moral cause.

GEORGIA, ALABAMA, AND MISSISSIPPI: THE HEART OF 1960S CIVIL RIGHTS PROTESTS

The civil rights movement was beginning to hit its stride in late 1961 and early 1962, infused with the energy and moral passion of its youthful participants. Another major battle occurred in Albany, Georgia, during that time. Local African Americans had long been active in combating racism there. They had sought voting rights and improvements in the conditions of their daily lives. SNCC activists came to the city and helped found the Albany Movement as a black coalition dedicated to ending segregation in the town. Mass meetings, street protests, and occupations of segregated facilities became the focus of the movement. By December 1961, protest leaders called on Martin Luther King to come to Albany to assist. Knowing that his presence would generate national publicity, King came to Albany and was promptly arrested and jailed.

Albany Police Chief Laurie Pritchett handled the protests far more expediently than other Southern officials. Although he made mass arrests, he dispersed the inmates to other counties and avoided the jail overcrowding and brutal incidents that had occurred in Alabama, Mississippi, and elsewhere. When Dr. King and Rev. Abernathy returned for sentencing in July 1962, they were jailed, but Pritchett arranged their release in secret. The mass actions resulted in few tangible victories.

The conventional view is that the Albany campaign was a serious defeat for Dr. King and the entire civil rights movement. That view, however, is overly simplistic. Despite its limited short-term successes, the Albany campaign continued, with the collective work of people on the ground. The movement learned, among other things, about the extraordinary power of music in social actions with the SNCC Freedom Singers, the value of long-term persistence, and the capacity to adjust its strategies and tactics to specific conditions and circumstances. SNCC organizers and local activists remained in the area and protested racism in nearby communities. They continued to register black voters and the following spring caused the city commission to repeal the segregation laws. Broad-based civil rights action, if not as dramatic as the Montgomery boycott of 1955–1956, was an enduring key to success in Albany and elsewhere.

SNCC Freedom Singers

Demonstrations continued throughout the South while many white politicians cynically exploited the tensions of the era to reinforce their hold on white voters who responded to naked racist appeals. The most dramatic example occurred in Mississippi in 1962, when Air Force veteran James Meredith sought to become the first African American to attend the University of Mississippi. He had applied to "Ole Miss" several times before and had been rejected on racial grounds. He sued and eventually the Supreme Court ruled that he was entitled to be admitted.

James Meredith

Governor Ross Barnett, however, attempted to stop his admission, even personally intervening to prevent his enrollment. Barnett made several inflammatory racist speeches throughout the state, appealing to the worst instincts of his electoral base. Like Arkansas Governor Orval Faubus in 1957, Barnett set up a major confrontation with the federal government when he defied a federal court order. President John Kennedy, concerned about his reelection prospects with white voters in 1964, tried negotiating with Barnett, seeking desperately to avoid using federal troops.

These negotiations failed, and Kennedy finally had no alternative but to deploy the superior force of the federal government. He federalized the Mississippi National Guard to quell the riots that had broken out on the University of Mississippi campus. Two people were killed and many more were injured and arrested; property damage was severe. But on October 1, 1962, James Meredith became the first black student to enroll at the University of Mississippi. Despite ongoing harassment and isolation, he managed to become the first black graduate of Ole Miss in 1963.

That year was also one of the most tumultuous in modern American history. The Southern Christian Leadership Conference decided to focus its fight against Jim Crow in Birmingham, Alabama, where SCLC leader Rev. Fred Shuttlesworth had spearheaded local civil rights activities. Birmingham was a bastion of segregation and racial violence, and many of its public officials were uncompromising in their refusal to abandon its racist culture and practices. The most intransigent of all was Public Safety Commissioner Eugene "Bull" Connor, who responded swiftly and brutally to civil rights demonstrations, as he had revealed during the 1961 freedom rides.

Eugene "Bull" Connor

Mass protests began in April. Dr. King ignored the injunction that authorities obtained and was quickly jailed. He had hoped that his arrest would catalyze an even more massive uprising. While incarcerated, Dr. King penned his famous "Letter from a Birmingham Jail," one of his most eloquent statements and a powerful argument for nonviolent civil disobedience and a compelling refutation of "gradual" racial change and "moderation" in the civil rights struggle. The demonstrations escalated, with hundreds of schoolchildren taking to the streets and then going to jail. These youthful foot soldiers now formed the backbone of the modern civil rights movement; without their committed participation, the Birmingham campaign would have faltered, slowing the entire movement for racial justice in the United States.

Bull Connor responded with predictable brutality. Using snarling police dogs and high-powered fire hoses, he drove back the youthful demonstrators, forcing the Kennedy Administration to act to reduce the crisis. Administration official pressured Birmingham civil and business leaders to make changes. Desiring an end to the massive disorder, they agreed to desegregate stores and to hire more African American workers in return for civil peace.

But the nation's attention was riveted to the extensive television images of fire hoses, police dogs, and naked police brutality—and the courage of young people willing, indeed eager, to go to jail for their principles. Millions of viewers became aware, many of them for the first time, of the barriers that African Americans faced and the seriousness of their efforts to secure change.

On June 11, 1963, President Kennedy made a speech on national television advocating congressional action on a civil rights bill that was more extensive than what he had earlier proposed. Street demonstrations—the power of the people—forced his hand, revealing the deeper impact of agitational action on the political process. Kennedy spoke forcefully, asserting that the quest for equal rights for black Americans was a moral issue and that the time had come for the nation to fulfill its promise to its African American citizens.

Byron De La Beckwith

Medgar Evers

Dr. King, his colleagues and aides, and thousands of civil rights workers were gratified by the president's words. But their exhilaration proved to be short-lived. In the early morning of June 12, Mississippi Field Secretary Medgar Evers was ambushed and assassinated by a white racist named Byron De La Beckwith. It would take another 30 years for authorities to finally convict him of this murder. Among many activists, the murder had a visceral impact, akin to the assassination of President Kennedy a few months later.

The Evers murder occurred in the midst of a gigantic increase in Southern civil rights activity. In the ten weeks following the Birmingham settlement, there were more than 750 demonstrations and almost 15,000 arrests in 186 communities. The wave of activity led various African American leaders to organize the massive March on Washington for Jobs and Freedom for August 28, 1963. The key figure was A. Philip Randolph, the planner of the threatened March on Washington in 1941. Now Randolph was joined by a coalition of civil rights organizations, including SNCC, SCLC, the NAACP, and the Urban League, as well as progressive labor unions and religious groups and clergy. More moderate civil rights leaders hoped the march would support President Kennedy's civil rights bill, while more militant participants saw it as an opportunity to generate even greater mass action

A. Philip Randolph

and to raise deeper issues of economic inequality. The president himself was noticeably cool, even oppositional, to the march, fearing adverse political consequences.

Longtime activist Bayard Rustin was the key logistical and mobilization figure for the march. The event itself was—and remains—unparalleled in American history. The administrative details were daunting. Transportation for buses and trains, selecting and training march marshals, arranging temporary housing, providing water and portable toilets, and a myriad other details were crucial to the march's success. Beyond all the highly visible features of this march and all the other successful civil rights demonstrations of the era, rigorous organization was critical.

Approximately 250,000 marchers, predominately but not exclusively black, converged on the nation's capital for the speeches and music. At the Lincoln Memorial, following a song by Odetta, actor Ossie Davis announced the death in Ghana of W.E.B. Du Bois the day before. Throughout the day, such other singers as Mahalia Jackson, the SNCC Freedom Singers, Bob Dylan, Joan Baez, Marian Anderson, and Peter, Paul and Mary entertained the audience.

The speakers were powerful, and all the major civil rights leaders had their turn: Roy Wilkins of the NAACP, Whitney Young of the Urban League, and Floyd McKissick of CORE, substituting for James Farmer, who was jailed in Louisiana. The march culminated in Dr. King's majestic "I Have a Dream Speech," which was actually a far deeper critique of American racial history and policy than out-of-context media excerpts have generally revealed for a half century. SNCC leader John Lewis, at the last moment, removed some of the more militant language from his speech to assuage march leaders of a more conservative, pro-Kennedy bent. National and international media coverage was extensive, further solidifying the prominence of the civil rights struggle at the forefront of American consciousness

But once again, the euphoria following the march was shattered by another monstrous act of racist violence. The Sixteenth Street Baptist Church in Birmingham, often a site of civil rights organizing, became a target after civil rights activists started a campaign for African American voter registration. On Sunday morning, May 15, a bomb exploded at the church, injuring several people and killing four young African American girls—Denise McNair, Addie Mae Collins, Carole Robertson, and Cynthia Wesley. America was reminded, yet again, of the huge barriers and the horrific human price of the long march toward freedom.

John F. Kennedy

Lyndon B. Johnson

The assassination of President John Kennedy in Dallas on November 22, 1963 was a national tragedy that also altered the trajectory of the civil rights movement. The elevation of Lyndon Johnson to the presidency solidified civil rights as the chief domestic issue in the United States. In his first address to Congress, President Johnson pledged to pass civil rights legislation and make it a monument to the martyred president. He asked Congress to expedite the bill and "eliminate from this nation every trace of discrimination and oppression that is based on race and color." Johnson was a shrewder legislative tactician than Kennedy. He had extensive experience as the Democratic leader in the Senate and was familiar with (indeed fond of) the use of power and personal persuasion to get what he wanted. Moreover, as a Texan, he had less to fear from his Southern colleagues than his Northern predecessor had.

Some civil rights leaders also began shifting their attention to voting rights, invoking the slogan "one man, one vote." This focus had been overshadowed by the highly publicized struggles to integrate schools, bus and train stations, restaurants, and other commercial establishments. Much of the focus was on Mississippi, with the formation of the umbrella organization Council of Federated Organizations (COFO), led by SNCC activist Robert Moses, who had arrived in the state in 1961. Moses organized schools to instruct local African Americans how to meet voter registration requirements, fully realizing that he had to recruit local people, especially in rural counties with large working-class populations to take an active leadership role in the process. One recruit was Fannie Lou Hamer, a daughter of sharecroppers whose powerful speaking and singing voice led her subsequently to key leadership roles in SNCC and the Mississippi Freedom Democratic Party (MFDP).

White resistance was concerted and vicious. In 1961, a Mississippi state legislator, who was acquitted by claiming "self-defense," murdered black farmer Herbert Lee, who tried to convince local blacks to participate in voter registration schools. Many other voter registration volunteers and prospective registrants were harassed, beaten, and jailed, including Fannie Lou Hamer, who was savagely attacked in a Montgomery County jail in 1963.

Fannie Lou Hamer

The most ambitious project in this campaign was the Freedom Summer of 1964, whose chief architect was Robert Moses. The goal was to recruit college students from throughout the United States to come to Mississippi to assist local African Americans in their civil rights struggles. The most important goal was to register as many African Americans to vote as possible, but several other activities were part of the broader Freedom Summer program. The recruitment process appealed to idealistic students, many of whom were white sympathizers who had seen civil rights events unfold on television screens for years. Organizers also knew that if white volunteers in Mississippi were arrested, injured, or killed, national attention and federal action would likely increase.

Organizers established a training site in Oxford, Ohio, where they learned about registering black voters, teaching in freedom schools, and promoting the Mississippi Freedom Democratic Party. A week after the arrival of the first volunteers in Oxford, Mississippi, another catastrophic act of racist violence occurred. Three SNCC volunteers, James Chaney, an African American Mississippian, and two white Jewish New Yorkers, Michael Schwerner and Andrew Goodman, were reported missing. They had been working to register black voters and had investigated a black church bombing.

James Chaney   Michael Schwerner   Andrew Goodman

Like many other activists, the three volunteers had been arrested and jailed on bogus charges. Upon their release, they were followed on the road by KKK operatives, who murdered them with the active complicity of law enforcement officials in Neshoba County. Their bodies were found 44 days later underneath a dam; Chaney had been beaten as well as shot. The disappearance of the civil rights workers was widely covered in the national media. President Johnson met with the parents of Goodman and Schwerner at the White House, and the grisly incident and the overall work of activists in the Freedom Summer project catalyzed the passage of Johnson's civil rights legislation.

The president signed the historic legislation on July 2, 1964. Many dignitaries, including Dr. King and other civil rights luminaries, were in attendance. The law was sweeping in its coverage and contained several anti-discrimination provisions, including education and employment, and declared the enforcement of constitutional rights as the national policy of the United States. The most important provision was the public accommodations section because much of the recent civil rights agitation against segregated facilities focused on this area.

Despite the primary focus of voter registration, Freedom Summer had only limited success—at least in terms of sheer numbers. Only 1600 African American voters were added to the rolls, but people were mobilized and the commitment to electoral empowerment deepened. The efforts in Mississippi during the summer of 1964 also led to increased pressure for national voting rights legislation.

SNCC organizers of Freedom Summer also created Freedom Schools, which brought long-needed educational services to many African Americans in the state. More than 3000 young and older black students attended freedom schools to learn basic mathematics and language skills as well as black history, the philosophy of the civil rights movement, and leadership principles. These new institutions supplemented the inadequate educational resources that African Americans had faced in Mississippi for generations. They served, moreover, as a model for the black and ethnic studies movement that developed throughout the country in the late 1960s.

One of the primary developments of Freedom Summer was the success of volunteers in making the MFDP a serious alternative to Mississippi's traditionally segregated Democratic Party. Established earlier in 1964 through COFO, it challenged the regular Democratic Party at the Atlantic City National Convention in August that nominated Lyndon Johnson for reelection. It wanted to unseat the "regulars" and substitute itself as the legitimate representative of all Mississippi Democrats.

President Johnson was adamantly opposed to the MFDP's attempt, even though 80,000 people, mostly black, had signed up with the insurgent party. Fannie Lou Hamer spoke passionately to the convention's credentials committee, but Johnson had

Fannie Lou Hamer

ONE MAN
FDP
ONE VOTE

the television stations break away for his own "emergency" speech. Finally, the official Democratic Party offered a compromise whereby the MFDP would have two seats at large, with no voting rights. Johnson deployed several operatives to try to impose his will, including Minnesota Senator Hubert Humphrey, his soon-to-be vice-presidential running mate.

MFDP leaders refused, however, realizing that this was another example in a long history of white men determining black representation and ignoring the other 62 ordinary Mississippi citizens who had journeyed to Atlantic City. Ignoring the pleas of liberal white politicians and even civil rights leaders like Martin Luther King and Bayard Rustin to accept the compromise as a moral victory, Hamer and others refused to be delegated yet again to second-class status. Their uncompromising stance helped pave the way for an even more intense drive for black voting rights in the South.

Early 1965 marked a dramatic development in the voting rights thrust of the civil rights movement. Focusing again on Alabama, Dr. King announced a major campaign for voting rights in Selma. SNCC had already been on the ground in Alabama on that issue, and tensions existed between the organizations based on ideology, organizational structure, and age. Still, both SCLC and SNCC were committed to the same objectives and worked in concert on the issue in Selma.

Alabama, like Mississippi, had an extremely low percentage of black voters. African American protests in Selma met with familiar police brutality, this time in the person of Sheriff Jim Clark. His brutality was comparable to that of Bull Connor in Birmingham. He wore a button that read "Never" and carried a cattle prod, club, and pistol, repeatedly threatening civil rights workers and jailing them at any provocation. Martin Luther King joined the demonstration on February 1 and was arrested at the Selma Courthouse. Following his arrest, hundreds of African Americans, including schoolchildren, joined the protests, leading to mass arrests.

Jimmy Lee Jackson

In nearby Marion, 26-year-old African American protestor Jimmy Lee Jackson was killed by a state police officer as he tried to protect his mother and grandfather, who were being beaten by state troopers. Shot on February 18, he died on February 26. His death catalyzed more protests, and SCLC leaders announced a march from Selma to the Alabama capitol in Montgomery to showcase the plight of African Americans in the state. Dr. King gave the eulogy at Jackson's funeral on March 3 and asked why the United States was concerned about Vietnam but ignored its own black citizens.

The events four days later, March 7, became a watershed moment in the civil rights movement. About 600 demonstrators, including John Lewis, commenced the march and attempted to cross the Edmund Pettus Bridge in Selma, on their way to Montgomery. The marchers encountered police commanded by Jim Clark and Major John Cloud, who ordered them to disperse. The marchers refused, bowing down in a prayerful gesture. The police attacked mercilessly with clubs and tear gas. Many of the marchers were injured, including Lewis, who sustained a fractured skull. Known as "Bloody Sunday," the incident was seen by millions of Americans on television, reminding them of the scarce progress of civil rights in racist bastions like Selma, Alabama.

Jim Clark

King led a symbolic march to the bridge two days later, and civil rights leaders sought a court order for a full-scale march to Montgomery. On March 10, approximately 1000 protestors confronted police outside Selma, knelt in prayer, and then returned to the church where they had begun. One of the demonstrators was Unitarian Minister James Reeb, who had come to Selma after seeing Bloody Sunday on television. He and two other white clergymen dined at an integrated restaurant and were later attacked by

James Reeb

several white men. Reeb was severely injured and, after brain surgery in Birmingham, died on March 11. No one was convicted of his murder. The national outcry was enormous, with thousands of people nationwide condemning the murder, many more than had protested the earlier slaying of Jimmy Lee Jackson.

On Sunday, March 21, the march from Selma to Montgomery began with over 25,000 participants. Civil rights activist celebrities like Harry Belafonte and Lena Horne joined in, heightening media interest in the event. The marchers arrived at the state capitol, where King and others spoke of the continuing need for voting rights legislation and federal assistance. After the march was over, another white volunteer horrified by Bloody Sunday, Viola Liuzzo, helped drive demonstrators back to their homes and colleges. As they were driving, Klan members ambushed them, pulled along the car, and shot Liuzzo, killing her instantly.

The Selma campaign had a major impact on national policy. President Johnson had

Viola Liuzzo

appeared on March 15 in a televised address before Congress, where he used the words "we shall overcome." He sent a voting rights bill to Congress two days later and, after a filibuster attempt, the legislation passed on July 9. President Johnson, recalling the outrage in Selma, signed the Voting Rights Act of 1965 on August 6, with Dr. King, Rosa Parks, and other civil rights figures in attendance. This landmark legislation finally implemented the 15th Amendment comprehensively.

In June 2013, however, the U.S. Supreme Court's conservative majority struck down Section 4 of the Act, the provision that designated which parts of the country required federal clearance for changes to their voting laws. The 5–4 decision in *Shelby County v. Holder* held that "things have changed dramatically since the Voting Rights Act." Congressman John Lewis, who had been seriously injured as an activist in Selma in 1965, said that Supreme Court had "put a dagger into the very heart of the Voting Rights Act."

By the time President Johnson signed the legislation, the civil rights movement had obtained many of its most cherished objectives. Segregated schools and public facilities were substantially gone, and voting rights for African Americans were confirmed, at least in theory. Freedom rides, sit-ins, the events in Albany, Birmingham, and Selma, the civil rights legislation—these were the highlights that made the black freedom struggle occupy center stage in the national and international news.

But there were many more protests that involved masses of ordinary African Americans seeking to remove racist practices that kept America from fulfilling its promise to its citizens of color and to implement its democratic principles. Most were only briefly noted nationally if at all, but all contributed to the modern civil rights crusade. In Louisiana, for example, civil rights sit-ins and other demonstrations occurred on New Orleans's historic Canal Street and in public buildings for years in the early 1960s. In

Plaquemine, CORE staged large demonstrations that were brutally suppressed and resulted in mass arrests. Many similar activities occurred in other Southern states.

1960S NORTHERN CIVIL RIGHTS PROTESTS

The civil rights movement was likewise a national movement, not confined at all to the South. Large demonstrations occurred across the East Coast and in Midwestern cities such as Chicago. California was a particular focus of militant nonviolent action, often attracting students with personal experience in the South.

The San Francisco Bay Area was an especially active location for civil rights agitation. With a large representation of politically engaged students from UC Berkeley and San Francisco State College and with large African American populations in San Francisco and Oakland, the region was ripe for rebellion.

A key focus was discriminatory hiring policies against African Americans. CORE targeted merchants in Berkeley and San Francisco in 1963 and 1964 and met with substantial success.

The largest protests occurred in San Francisco in 1964, when CORE and other activists took on the city's major hotels. Mass demonstrations were followed by legal actions and mass arrests. Comedian and activist Dick Gregory, a veteran of SNCC actions in Atlanta, joined the protests. After intervention by prominent local politicians, the hotels agreed to a nondiscriminatory hiring policy. The mainstream press, meanwhile, criticized the demonstrators, going so far as to make allegations of Communist influence reminiscent of the McCarthy era.

The Bay Area civil rights movement next targeted the major San Francisco car dealers. The same pattern repeated, with black and white participants arrested. The NAACP threatened nationwide demonstrations, and the auto dealers finally made substantial concessions.

Los Angeles was likewise a major site of 1960s civil rights activity. In 1963, the United Civil Rights Committee, a coalition of civil rights organizations, was formed to challenge discrimination in employment, education, and housing and police brutality. In June 1963, it organized what was then the largest civil rights march in Los Angeles history. It continued with several other marches that called public attention to continuing racism in the region. In 1964, it helped organize an unsuccessful attempt to stop repeal of the Rumford Fair Housing Act, against the larger political power of real estate interests.

CORE and its offshoot, the Nonviolent Action Committee, organized direct action campaigns against employment discrimination by Van de Kamp Bakeries, the Bank of America, and other enterprises. Pickets, marches, and arrests occurred regularly. Los Angeles police officers were frequently hostile and violent, while white hecklers were eerily similar in their verbal and physical assaults to those of the Deep South.

Even conservative San Diego had a thriving civil rights movement during the early and mid-1960s. CORE was the chief organization, targeting housing discrimination and the local real estate industry and employment discrimination at the San Diego Gas and Electric Company and the Bank of America. The latter was a statewide focus of CORE, with actions in Los Angeles and the Bay Area. In downtown San Diego, demonstrators were arrested at the Bank of America in June 1964, and several civil rights defendants were harshly treated in subsequent trials in the local municipal court.

As 1965 drew to a close, many Americans became increasingly preoccupied by the escalating war in Vietnam, the major factor of the failed Lyndon Johnson presidency. Some whites and even some African Americans had come to believe that the civil rights movement had won and that it was largely over. The dramatic reemergence of black nationalism, however, ensured that the African American freedom struggle would remain front and center in national political life.

Chapter 5:

THE RESURGENCE OF BLACK NATIONALISM AND DEVELOPMENT OF BLACK POWER

The magnificent advances of the 1960s civil rights movement allowed African American school children and university students to attend integrated schools, enabled African Americans to eat and shop wherever they chose, and helped them obtain employment where they formerly had been excluded. The movement even registered many African Americans to vote, and they became a significant electoral force throughout the nation, including various Southern locales. But it would have been seriously wrong to declare victory.

The economic position of ordinary African Americans remained largely static. Black income remained among the lowest in the nation, and violence—including police brutality—against African Americans and other people of color remained a daily reality. Millions of black people continued to live in poor inner-city areas with inferior public and private services and declining schools. Racial problems hardly disappeared after 1965, and neither did the civil rights movement.

Severe black frustration and anger resulted in major urban uprisings, referred to as "riots" in the news media and educational materials, throughout the decade. The disturbances resulted in extensive property damage, injuries, fatalities, and rampant lawlessness, as well as brutal responses by the police and military forces called in to quell them. Such outbursts occurred in New York City in 1964; Rochester, New York, in 1964; Philadelphia in 1964; Los Angeles in 1965; Newark in 1967; Detroit in 1967; and Washington, D.C., in 1968, among other cities.

A 1970 shooting incident in the Marin County Courthouse in California, where black radical Jonathan Jackson tried to negotiate freedom for the Soledad Brothers from nearby San Quentin Prison (where they allegedly killed a prison guard but were later acquitted), evoked major national publicity when four people died, including Jackson and Judge Harold Haley. Black radical Angela Davis was arrested and charged as an accomplice in the shooting incident, but she was later found not guilty. The 1971 Attica prison uprising in New York State, resulting in a massacre of prisoners ordered by Governor Nelson Rockefeller, followed on the heels of these traumatic events and presaged ongoing black grievances about incarceration in the United States. The urban uprisings and the incidents in Marin County and Attica fueled black rebellion and added impetus to the drive for Black Power and nationalism.

Jonathan Jackson

The overall focus and direction of civil rights activity thus changed, assuming a more militant and radical tone. Many of the new figures in the emerging racial struggles were younger veterans

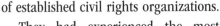

of established civil rights organizations. They had experienced the most dramatic battles and were seasoned community organizers. Now they began to articulate a new vision, calling for greater black empowerment, leadership, and racial pride, articulated in the slogan "Black Power." Earlier commitments to nonviolence began to give way to visions of self-defense and even armed revolt. The violent confrontations that rocked major American cities as the 1960s progressed both deepened greater racial polarization and intensified the spirit of black nationalist rebellion.

Many historians and social commentators point to a separation between the nonviolent civil rights movement of the early to mid-1960s and the subsequent Black Power movement. But a closer examination reveals that the later developments reflect a continuation of the same basic struggle. The preceding phase of the civil rights movement in mid-decade created the context for the new militant phase, which focused on the long-neglected needs of the urban black poor and others for whom the breakdown of legal segregation was valuable but inadequate.

Although some civil rights activists were troubled by the new rhetoric, many, perhaps even most, came to understand that black political power and economic development were the logical next steps. Dr. Martin Luther King, despite some initial doubts, incorporated a stronger and more radical economic message in his activism. His vision, especially at time of his tragic murder in 1968, was actually much closer to that of the militant Black Power leaders than the media portrayed. Popular accounts, persisting into the early 21st century, that posit Martin Luther King as the "good black" and Black Power figures as Afro-wearing, gun-wielding, white-hating Black Panthers and fanatic Malcolm X followers are patently misleading.

The new black militancy of the mid- and late 1960s had long historical roots in America. Rebel slaves and radical abolitionists were legitimate precursors of the Black Power movement. In the early 20th century, Marcus Garvey's UNIA movement, for all its organizational and other problems, generated similar racial pride among working-class blacks that new militants like Malcolm X, the Black Panthers, and others could generate many decades later. The Communist Party likewise generated a radical vision that often had a robust influence among some African Americans. Its Marxist critique of capitalism generally resonated with black activists of the late 1960s and 1970s by incorporating a class as well as a racial analysis in its call for structural change.

Several prominent contemporary African American figures also deeply influenced the militant new phase of the civil rights/freedom struggle. Foremost among them was Paul Robeson, who devoted his entire adult life as an artist and political activist to a powerful vision of liberation for all oppressed people, nationally and internationally. That vision was rooted in his black racial identification, expressed in the opening lines of his 1958 memoir and political manifesto, *Here I Stand*: "I am a Negro. The house I live in is in Harlem—this city within a city. . . . " In the book, Robeson expressed his strong identification with Africa and Third World peoples of color, promoting an aggressive strategy for black liberation in America and for black leadership. Each of these principles found significant expression during the height of the black nationalist revival.

Paul Robeson

Robeson's views on self-defense also struck a responsive chord with Black Power adherents. In a 1947 meeting with President Harry

Truman about the continuing problem of lynching, he told the president that if the federal government refused to defend black citizens, blacks would have to defend themselves—a statement that would presage the comments of Malcolm X during the early 1960s. That position, perhaps as much as anything else, revealed Black Power's radical departure from Martin Luther King's pacifist approach to racial justice.

Robeson's friend and close political ally, W.E.B. Du Bois, whose roots in earlier civil rights struggles made him a highly venerated figure among the younger activists, was also a major influence on the new black militancy. His longtime intellectual and activist record and his powerful Pan-African perspective pervaded the ideological focus of many Black Power advocates in the late 1960s and 1970s. Du Bois joined such other intellectual theorists as C.L.R. James, George Padmore, and Frantz Fanon and African liberation leaders such as Jomo Kenyatta, Kwame Nkrumah, martyred Patrice Lumumba, and others as inspirations of the new American black militants.

MALCOLM X

The most iconic figure associated with black nationalism in the United States was Malcolm X. Throughout his later life and for many years after

Malcolm X

his assassination in 1965, he was demonized in conventional media as the angry black demagogue who hated whites and wanted nothing more than black separatism. He was typically juxtaposed with Martin Luther King, the good and noble leader (who, in fact, was also widely reviled during his lifetime). After the posthumous publication of Alex Haley's more comprehensive if sentimental *The Autobiography of Malcolm X*, the public found a more nuanced and sympathetic treatment of this major figure in 20th century African American history. Spike Lee's 1992 biopic and later scholarly treatments by Michael Dyson, Victor Wolfenstein, Manning Marable, and others countered the simplistic earlier portrayals of Malcolm, offering new insights into his leading role as a proponent of the African American freedom struggle.

The trajectory of Malcolm's life is well known, from his early days as a street hustler, his time in prison and conversion to the Nation of Islam (NOI/Black Muslims), and his emergence as a charismatic religious and political leader. That emergence included his early work with NOI and his black nationalist organizing, speeches, and writings, his break with Black Muslim leader Elijah Muhammad, his trips to Africa and Mecca, his formation of the Organization of Afro-American Unity, and his assassination on February 21, 1965.

Malcolm X had a voice and vision that spoke directly to the most marginalized members of the African American community. Like Garvey before him, he spoke to people who knew unemployment, welfare, incarceration, and rank indifference or worse from the white majority. Unlike Dr. King, whose roots were solidly upper-middle-class, Malcolm came from and understood the "black street." His message of black consciousness reflected the idea that black people were not and could never be defined as victims of racism, but instead were destined for greatness based on the rich heritage of their African past. This nationalist, Pan-African perspective had a major influence on the development of Black Power ideology, as Stokely Carmichael acknowledged.

Malcolm's specific political statements were directly contrary to those of most mainstream civil rights organizations and leaders. In one of his last speeches as a Black Muslim, "Message to the Grassroots" in November 1963 in Detroit, he essentially called for black revolution. In the speech, he charismatically combined the rhetoric of self-defense and anti-colonialism with a mocking critique of many contemporary blacks, using his famous distinction of "house Negroes and field Negroes" to drive home the point.

After leaving the NOI, Malcolm further refined his political philosophy. In his April 1964 speech "The Ballot or the Bullet," his nationalist perspective emerged clearly. Speaking at a church in Cleveland, Malcolm called for blacks to control the politics and economics of their own communities and to use the ballot strategically for genuine political change. He also reiterated his advocacy of self-defense, justifying the appeal for violence: "Where the government has proven itself unwilling or unable to defend the lives and property of Negroes," he declared, "it's time for Negroes to defend themselves."

Malcolm continued his political activity, shadowed by NOI attacks and threats of death from his enemies. Near the end of his life, in the months before his murder, his social and political vision expanded even further. Now it included people of different races and nationalities, as he became open to a more global vision of radical political transformation.

Many observers today like to regard Malcolm X as little different from Martin Luther King, undergoing a transformation following his trip to Mecca that turned him into a humanist and integrationist. Like the earlier caricatures, this, too, is simplistic. As biographer Manning Marable argues, Malcolm always saw himself, like Paul Robeson, as black man living in America. He was a black nationalist *and* an internationalist, who linked the black struggle in America to the broader campaign against colonialism and imperialism. His commitment, above all, was to his people, a vision that played a powerful role in the values and practices of the women, men, and movements that followed him after his tragic death.

The Black Power and nationalist crusade in the aftermath of the civil rights struggles and triumphs of the late 1950s to mid-1960s was far from a unified movement. Like its nonviolent predecessors, it had several strains and many conflicts, some of which resulted in hostility and violence. Some of the differences were ideological and some were personal; all were exacerbated by concerted governmental repression against various black militant groups, especially by the Federal Bureau of Investigation and local police throughout the country.

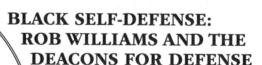

Robert F. Williams

BLACK SELF-DEFENSE: ROB WILLIAMS AND THE DEACONS FOR DEFENSE

Although the Black Power focus emerged largely after the most significant civil rights victories of the early to mid-1960s, there is no simple, linear timeline for this more aggressive approach. There had been earlier voices. One powerful early figure was Robert F. (Rob) Williams, whose eloquent 1954 comments about the impact of *Brown v. Board of Education* reflected national African American sentiment. He was active and controversial at the same time that King and others were more prominent in national consciousness and public recognition.

In 1955, Williams returned to Monroe, North Carolina, and assumed a leadership role in the NAACP. Monroe had a strong KKK presence, and Williams fought a series of battles with local racists, encouraging fellow African Americans to return gunfire. The national NAACP suspended him for six months because of his strong disagreement with organizational leadership.

Williams also took strong issue with King's commitment to nonviolence. Following a confrontation with the Klan in which Williams brought a white couple to his home to keep them safe from angry fellow blacks, he was charged with kidnapping and fled the country. Eventually landing in Cuba, he published a book in 1962, *Negroes With Guns*, that advocated armed self-defense. The tract was to have a powerful influenced on the Black Panthers and other black militants. It also won respect among many civil rights volunteers, who, while practicing nonviolence because it was a powerful and effective strategy that gained national respect, were not the fully committed pacifists that Martin Luther King and his colleagues were. In exile, Rob Williams made radical broadcasts on a program from Havana called Radio Free Dixie.

Rob Williams was not alone in rejecting Gandhi's pacifist vision. In Louisiana, in 1964, a group of African American men formed the Deacons for Defense and Justice to protect CORE members against KKK violence. The Deacons were a self-defense force that worked discreetly, keeping their membership and even their existence a secret. The group provided security for civil rights activists and the African American population generally, mostly in Louisiana but also in Alabama and Mississippi.

Deacons for Defense

Although they departed from the nonviolent orthodoxy of the mainstream civil rights movement at the time, the Deacons represented a long strain of black willingness to resort to force in defense of their physical safety and their ideals.

STOKELY CARMICHAEL, SNCC, AND THE BLACK PANTHER PARTY

Another giant figure emerging from the earlier days of the modern civil rights movement was Stokely Carmichael, a leading Black Power spokesperson with roots in the Student Nonviolent Coordinating Committee. Carmichael had been a freedom rider and had been imprisoned at the notorious Parchman Penitentiary, had done outstanding voter registration work in Mississippi, and had become an effective community organizer and public speaker. After being elected SNCC chairman, he turned the organization in a more radical direction.

The spark of Carmichael's transition to Black Power was a march in Mississippi after the shooting of James Meredith during his solitary walk through the state in June 1966. Prominent civil rights figures including Rev. King, Floyd McKissick, and Carmichael continued Meredith's protest against racism, dubbed the March Against Fear. Carmichael was arrested during the march and introduced the concept of Black Power in a speech upon his release from jail. For him, the phrase was a plea to African Americans to unite and build their own political, economic, social, and cultural institutions. For many in the white media, it was a "racist" slogan, a dangerous departure from the dignity of the older civil rights figures.

SNCC began to change significantly in the aftermath of Carmichael's Black Power proclamation. It distanced itself from the other civil rights

Stokely Carmichael

organizations, suffered serious internal conflicts, and excluded its white participants, though a handful remained. Carmichael himself indicated that white volunteers should focus their energy on their own communities and work to rid them of their deep-seated racism. He also urged them to organize among the white poor, eventually creating a strong coalition between poor blacks and whites. Carmichael's successor as the head of SNCC, H. Rap Brown, took the militant rhetoric a step further, saying, "violence is as American as apple pie." SNCC became a target of the FBI's Counterintelligence Program (COINTELPRO) and was weakened by internal conflicts and loss of financial backing. It faded into obscurity during the 1970s, albeit with a proud legacy of militant struggle and accomplishment.

Stokely Carmichael followed a radical path for the rest of his life. He opposed the Vietnam War, affiliated himself with the Black Panther Party, and spoke vigorously on behalf of black nationalism and international leftist movements. Changing his name to Kwame Ture, he moved to Africa (primarily Guinea) for most of the rest of his life and was active in the All-African People's Revolutionary Party.

Bobby Seale

Huey P. Newton

Just as Malcolm X was the most visible black nationalist figure of the 1950s and 1960s, the Black Panther Party (BPP) was the most prominent Black Power organization from its inception in 1966 to its demise in the mid-1970s. Founded by Huey Newton and Bobby Seale in Oakland, it was also demonized as a band of revolutionary zealots dedicated to destroying society, engaging in senseless violence, and causing discord in African American political life. Like the mainstream view of Malcolm X, such portrayals of the Black Panthers were (and still remain) extremely simplistic and prevented a more comprehensive public understanding of the historic role and contributions of the party throughout its existence. Although the Black Panthers were riddled with factional disputes and attracted some problematic elements, they reflected the widespread rage of millions of black youth and provided valuable community services that governmental officials had ignored for generations.

Throughout its relatively short existence, the Black Panther Party attracted men and women who would become significant historical figures in the period following the gains of the nonviolent civil rights movement. In addition to Newton and Seale, such notables as Stokely Carmichael, James Forman, Angela Davis, Elaine Browne, Eldridge Cleaver, Kathleen Cleaver, and Erika Huggins all played prominent roles in party activities. Some of these activists remained active into the early 21st century.

Newton and Seale got the name Black Panthers from the Lowndes County Freedom Organization in Alabama. This was a black political party in a white-controlled county with a majority black population that Carmichael and SNCC created in 1966 with a black panther as its emblem. Newton and Seale had read Fanon, Malcolm X, and Rob Williams along with various Marxist theorists, setting the ideological tone for their activities. One of the original objectives of the BPP was to patrol black neighborhoods to protect residents against police harassment and brutality, an acute problem in Oakland at the time. Ensconced in the poor African American neighborhoods of that city, the Panthers, with their black leather jackets, berets, and scarves, shadowed the police, often intimidating them to back away from their threats to arrest black citizens.

One of the BPP's initial acts was to lay out its agenda, a ten-point program designated "What We Want" and "What We Believe." The demands sounded radical, as much in tone as in substance, but most were fully in keeping with those pursued by the earlier civil rights movement—decent housing, better education that incorporated genuine African American history, the end of police brutality, and full employment for black people. Among the more revolutionary demands were calls for the release of black prisoners, an exemption for black men from military service, and a UN-supervised plebiscite for African Americans to determine their national destiny.

The BPP also published a weekly newspaper, *The Black Panther*, which reflected the leaders' ideological vision, often in provocative language reflecting the militancy of the movement. The paper also contained artwork, stories of international rebellion, and critiques of institutional power that contributed further to the party's aggressive, revolutionary reputation. While this attracted young black adherents in Oakland and elsewhere, it also attracted law enforcement scrutiny that would eventually have devastating consequences.

In May 1967, the Black Panthers made headlines when an armed contingent of 30 men and women went to the California State Capitol building in Sacramento. They were there to protest legislation that would ban the open display of weapons, aimed directly at them. Covered extensively in the national media, the incident propelled the BPP into a leadership position in the growing Black Power movement.

The Sacramento "invasion" also attracted other high-profile African American figures into its ranks. A temporary merger with SNCC brought Stokely Carmichael, H. Rap Brown, and James Forman to the BPP. One of the most celebrated recruits was Eldridge Cleaver, a

Eldridge Cleaver

felon since his teen years who became a black nationalist while in prison. His highly celebrated book in 1968, *Soul on Ice*, was widely read in black and white radical circles, with strong approval for its angry vision of racism and black masculinity. Widely overlooked was the pervasive sexism of Cleaver's screed, an issue and practice that would ultimately jeopardize the Panthers and that would exacerbate tensions between the African American liberation and women's liberation movements.

The BPP's conflicts with law-enforcement authorities escalated dramatically on October 28, 1967, when Newton was pulled over by Oakland police officer John Frey. The ensuing shootout injured Newton and killed Frey under ambiguous circumstances. Newton was indicted for murder. The Panthers made the "Free Huey" campaign into a cause célèbre that resonated with black militants and white radicals throughout the country. The BPP used the poster of Huey Newton wearing a black beret, sitting on a wicker chair, and holding a spear, as a powerful fund-raising image; it became one of the iconic Black Power portraits of the entire era. In September 1968, Newton was convicted of voluntary manslaughter and sentenced to prison.

The campaign surrounding Newton facilitated the BPP's expansion to other U.S. cities. By 1968, there were branches in Chicago, Boston, Los Angeles, New York, Newark, San Francisco, Philadelphia, Washington, and elsewhere. As membership grew, the party was recognized as the leading Black Power organization in the nation. One of its greatest impacts was to politicize and radicalize urban black youth, turning thousands into a potent force that the government could scarcely ignore.

In early 1969, the Black Panther Party began its community-service activities in earnest. Starting out with a free-breakfast program for children, it expanded into free health-care clinics, transportation for relatives of prisoners, and alternative schools stressing martial arts and liberation politics.

These were activities with highly practical human consequences—hungry elementary school pupils cannot learn if they are hungry—that reflected the BPP's vision of a more humane, equitable social order. Social programs remain one of the major and still under-acknowledged legacies of the entire Panther enterprise.

The year 1969 was also a time of crisis for the Black Panther Party. Continued conflicts with police and intense federal scrutiny and harassment combined with deep internal divisions and purges within the organization to intensify its problems. The high-profile murders in 1969 of Panther members Bunchy Carter and John Huggins in Los Angeles and of Fred Hampton and Mark Clark by police in Chicago exacerbated the existing strains within the party. Eldridge Cleaver and Bobby Seale faced their own legal problems while Newton was still in prison. Earlier mass arrests and criminal prosecutions in New York and New Haven in 1969 also weakened the BPP structure.

Internal sexism was another contradiction in the Black Panther Party, although its formal principles promoted the role of women. Elaine Brown, in fact, became party chair in 1974 after Newton's release from prison and his decision to flee to Cuba. The BPP entered electoral politics in Oakland, unsuccessfully running Brown for city council and Bobby Seale for mayor. The party lived on through the 1970s, albeit in significant decline from its previous strength. Its legacy, though mixed, extended the earlier civil rights

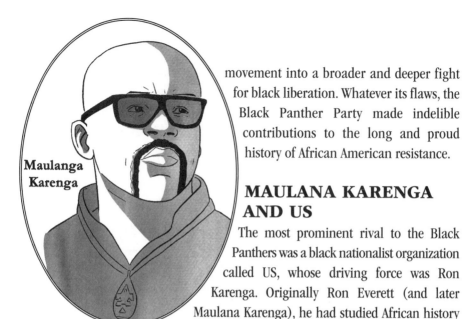

Maulanga Karenga

movement into a broader and deeper fight for black liberation. Whatever its flaws, the Black Panther Party made indelible contributions to the long and proud history of African American resistance.

MAULANA KARENGA AND US

The most prominent rival to the Black Panthers was a black nationalist organization called US, whose driving force was Ron Karenga. Originally Ron Everett (and later Maulana Karenga), he had studied African history and culture, which served as the foundation for his Afrocentric vision. As a student, he became deeply involved in studying African-related subjects, developing a lifelong commitment to a black nationalist perspective that gave rise to the creation of US (as opposed to "Them").

US members, like Karenga, assumed Swahili names and dressed in African garb. Their rituals were designed to promote African identity. Like the Universal Negro Improvement Association and the Nation of Islam, US had a highly authoritarian structure with carefully structured rituals and specifically ordered roles for members, especially women. Karenga, like Marcus Garvey and Elijah Muhammad, also engendered a strong cult of personality.

Kwanzaa

A key feature of the organization's value system was Kwanzaa, which Karenga established in 1965 as the first uniquely African-American holiday. Still widely celebrated today, its seven unifying principles serve as an alternative to traditional Christian and Jewish winter holidays in America.

US became a major rival, especially in Los Angeles, of the Black Panther Party. Each claimed to represent the vanguard of black revolution, but the differences were clear. Newton and the BPP regarded Karenga and US as mere cultural nationalists whose African dress, language, rituals, and the like were promoted at the expense of a rigorous political critique. For the BPP, US and what it represented negated political transformation. US, on the other hand, mistrusted the Panthers' alliance with white radicals and their commitment to a Marxist understanding of capitalism.

Turf wars in Los Angeles, reflecting in part the experience of former gang members in both organizations, led to a 1969 shootout at UCLA that resulted in the deaths of two Black Panthers. Retaliatory violence ensued, and the FBI used its power to escalate the conflicts. Karenga was imprisoned on assault charges in 1971, and US disbanded a few years later. After his release on parole in 1975, Karenga became a leading Afrocentric academic and denied criminal wrongdoing.

Although the resurgence of black nationalism and the promotion of Black Power from the mid- to late 1960s onward hardly altered the basic structure of power and the dynamics of race in America, it had lasting implications with positive consequences well into the 21st century. Above all, it gave African Americans, especially in urban ghettos, a renewed sense of pride, dignity, and hope. Among the most enduring concrete results were true educational advances in the wake of black nationalism and power. One of the early demands of the BPP and other groups was for a curriculum that would truly incorporate a comprehensive vision of black accomplishments in world and U.S. history.

That demand took an activist turn in the form of student demonstrations and takeovers calling for the creation of Black Studies programs and departments. Militant African American students, often organized into Black Student unions and similar organizations, along with many white and other allies, picketed, sat in, and went to jail to communicate their demand for fundamental curricular change. Major eruptions at San Francisco State College, Cornell University, the University of California at Berkeley, and many other institutions helped establish Black Studies units only after considerable agitation.

Political pressure for Black Studies emerged substantially from the most militant members of the African American community. University administrators, mostly male and mostly white, reluctantly gave in to the pressure. As with the transportation officials in Montgomery in 1956 and restaurant proprietors throughout the South, political force rather than moral suasion carried the day, compelling change and racial justice. As a result, most U.S. colleges and universities today have thriving African American Studies departments that have made distinguished contributions in education, scholarship, and public service for more than 40 years.

The impact of the new black militancy also had enduing effects on the arts. Organized black arts protests, with significant participation from black nationalist and Black Power groups and individuals, were held in many U.S. cities. Artists in New York, Los Angeles, and other locales with large numbers of African American cultural workers demanded both recognition and institutions for the dissemination and exhibition of their creative work. In Los Angeles, for example, the influence both of the Black Panthers and Karenga's US Organization led, at least in part, to the political impetus for creating black-controlled venues promoting black art in the city. Like African American Studies units in higher education, these institutions continue to survive into the early 21st century, resonating the tumultuous but vibrant period following the nonviolent civil rights era.

Chapter 6:

THE EXPRESSIVE CULTURE OF THE CIVIL RIGHTS MOVEMENT

The modern civil rights movement generated artistic and cultural expressions that both emerged from and contributed to African American freedom and resistance activities. A vast body of music, literature, visual art, and film dealing with the historical and more recent struggles for black liberation and dignity has been created, both by African Americans and their supporters from other racial and ethnic backgrounds. These creative products have traditionally been viewed alone, outside the political and social conflicts from which they emerged. But they have been a central part of the broad civil rights movements highlighted in this volume. They are much more than mere adjuncts to the cause; indeed, they are integral features of the movements themselves. Without these powerful and engaging expressions, whatever successes have been achieved would have been diminished, sometimes substantially.

Some of these cultural products have played a powerful role during the modern civil rights protests themselves. This is especially so for music, with many songs written and performed during the height of the movement in the 1960s. Other cultural products were created during the movement and afterwards, serving both as historical documentation and as impetus for further activism. What follows is a necessarily selective and limited sample of the range of civil rights music, literature, film, and visual arts that contributed to the movement both concurrently and subsequently.

MUSIC

Music has played a vital role in African American life. Negro spirituals have long been a potent expression of black religious faith, but they were much more than that alone. Some spirituals expressed resistance to slavery and oppression; some served as coded messages to slaves attempting to escape bondage.

Roland Hayes

First brought to wide public attention by the Fisk Jubilee Singers in the 1870s, they became fundamental features of American popular culture in the 20th century when Roland Hayes, Marian Anderson, and Paul Robeson featured them in major concert performances in the United States and throughout the world. Owing partly to the influence of Hayes, Anderson, and Robeson, these songs added a vital musical dimension to the modern civil rights movement from the mid-1950s through the early 1970s.

Mirian Anderson

114

Even this renaissance of politically engaged music had multiple roots. Few civil rights activists of the 1960s were unaware, for example, of Billie Holliday's haunting 1939 anti-racist song "Strange Fruit." Indeed, throughout the civil rights and Black Power era, sometimes fierce debates raged over what kinds of music, literature, and art most authentically represented the black community. These controversies have continued in academic circles to the present day.

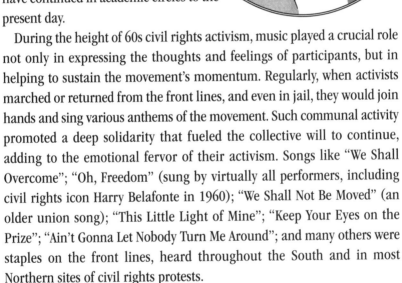

Billie Holiday

During the height of 60s civil rights activism, music played a crucial role not only in expressing the thoughts and feelings of participants, but in helping to sustain the movement's momentum. Regularly, when activists marched or returned from the front lines, and even in jail, they would join hands and sing various anthems of the movement. Such communal activity promoted a deep solidarity that fueled the collective will to continue, adding to the emotional fervor of their activism. Songs like "We Shall Overcome"; "Oh, Freedom" (sung by virtually all performers, including civil rights icon Harry Belafonte in 1960); "We Shall Not Be Moved" (an older union song); "This Little Light of Mine"; "Keep Your Eyes on the Prize"; "Ain't Gonna Let Nobody Turn Me Around"; and many others were staples on the front lines, heard throughout the South and in most Northern sites of civil rights protests.

The women, men, and children of the movement—the same people who formed the army of resistance that changed American history—often performed these freedom songs spontaneously. They made up in enthusiasm and passion what they may have lacked in formal musical training and education, though many revealed considerable natural talent. At the same time, professional singers also regularly performed the music of the civil rights movement, bringing that profound expression to millions of people throughout the world.

One of the key figures was Guy Carawan (1927–2015), a white folk musician who introduced "We Shall Overcome" to the founding convention of SNCC in 1960. Widely regarded as *the* anthem of the movement, this song is inextricably identified with the broader struggle for human rights beyond the African American cause. Thousands of civil rights workers have indelible memories of linking hands and singing the final lyrics: "Deep in my heart, I do believe, that we shall overcome some day." Carawan was long associated with the Highlander Folk School, where both Martin Luther King and Rosa Parks attended workshops. He worked tirelessly in the civil rights movement, singing, teaching, and documenting the socially conscious music of an entire activist generation.

Guy Carawan

Pete Seeger (1919–2014) was another iconic white folksinger whose political songs inspired civil rights activists, especially during the most tumultuous struggles of the 1960s. Seeger, whose long and distinguished career embraced numerous progressive causes, learned "We Shall Overcome" at the Highlander Folk School in the 1940s and actually changed the word "will" in the title to "shall," while adding various of his own verses. In 1963, Seeger performed and recorded a live concert at New York's Carnegie Hall, titled "We Shall Overcome," that both reflected and augmented the dramatic civil rights vigor of that time. At the

Pete Seeger

historic concert, Seeger sang such other inspirational songs as "If You Miss Me at the Back of the Bus," "Keep Your Eyes on the Prize," and his own creation, "I Ain't Scared of Your Jail." He was universally regarded in the movement as an effective and influential musical advocate for racial justice.

Odetta Holmes

Widely regarded as the premier voice of the civil rights movement, Odetta (Odetta Holmes, 1930–2008) was an acclaimed gospel, spiritual, and folk singer and an active participant in the campaign. Her presence at various marches and protests, like that of celebrity vocalists like Harry Belafonte, helped bring additional media attention to the black freedom struggle. When Odetta sang classics like "We Shall Overcome" and "Oh, Freedom," her passion had a profound emotional effect on audiences and motivated them to action. Odetta's impact was comparable to that of Marian Anderson at her historic Lincoln Memorial Concert in 1939. Like Anderson, she used spirituals to highlight her people's long march from slavery to freedom, using her magnificent voice to express the aspirations of her people for liberation from historical and modern oppression.

The SNCC Freedom Singers emerged directly from the civil rights movement itself. The Student Nonviolent Coordinating Committee formed the group in Albany, Georgia, in the midst of the campaign there in 1962. Its founder was Cordell Hull Reagon, and other original members were Bernice Johnson (later Dr. Bernice Johnson Reagon), Matthew Jones, Charles Neblett, and Ruth Harris, all of whom were African American SNCC activists with extensive frontline experience.

Freedom Singers

They used their music to raise funds for SNCC's organizing efforts, to spread the word of the civil rights movement, and to unite blacks and their allies in the cause.

The Freedom Singers sang a wide variety of freedom songs, including the most well-known ballads and newer compositions that condemned racist politicians like Alabama Governor George Wallace and commemorated martyrs like Medgar Evers. Pete Seeger made joint appearances with the group, giving them greater national visibility. The SNCC Freedom Singers traveled widely throughout the country, appearing in churches, colleges, and rallies. Their highlight came in August 1963, when they sang at the March on Washington. The group disbanded in 1963 after recording a single album ("We Shall Overcome"); an all-male successor group called the New Freedom Singers was created under the SNCC banner. Bernice Johnson Reagon went on to found Sweet Honey in the Rock, an all-female ensemble that has regularly focused on civil rights, racism, feminist, and other human rights issues in its long and storied history.

Staple Singers

The Staple Singers, featuring African American lead singer Mavis Staples (1939–), likewise added to the burgeoning body of music during the height of 60s civil rights activism. In 1963, the group presented a concert with Dr.

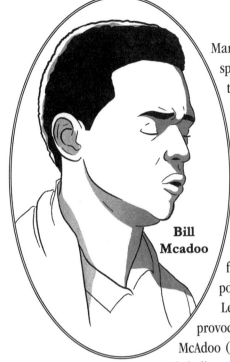

Bill Mcadoo

Martin Luther King in attendance. After speaking with him following the performance, the group changed its musical direction and wrote and performed songs specifically in support of the civil rights movement. Among other racial themes, the Staple Singers used their talent to provide commentary about the heroic Little Rock Nine and the 1965 Selma to Montgomery March. Like those of other musicians, their efforts fortified the will of activists and fueled the movement through passionate and politically engaged creative expression.

Lesser known, but equally talented and provocative, was African American folksinger Bill McAdoo (1936–2003). In his early twenties, McAdoo recorded albums that added a militant tone to the music of the civil rights era. Accompanied by Pete Seeger on the guitar, McAdoo wrote and performed "I'm Going to Walk and Talk for My Freedom," which celebrated the civil rights demonstrators in the South, and "I Don't Want No Jim Crow Coffee," which highlighted the historic 1960 Greensboro sit-in. The latter song also condemned racism in American labor unions, another thematic dimension of his repertoire. McAdoo later became a Black Studies academic at SUNY Stony Brook, a further feature of his lifelong civil rights commitment.

Several younger white performers of the era likewise stood out for their commitment to the civil rights movement and for their exceptionally creative contributions to the musical culture of the times. Bob Dylan (1941–), one of the most acclaimed singer-songwriters of the contemporary era, regularly addressed civil rights in the early part of his career. As a young man,

Bob Dylan

he wrote and performed several songs with dramatic anti-racist themes. One of his early recordings, "Oxford Town" in 1962, examined the violent confrontation between the federal government and Mississippi's racist authorities over the admission of James Meredith to the previously all-white University of Mississippi.

That same year, Dylan wrote and sang "Blowin' in the Wind." Popularized by Peter, Paul, and Mary and other performers, the song swiftly became another major anthem of the civil rights movement. One of the most influential socially conscious songs of all time, it has been recorded by scores of performers and sung at protest events of all kinds over the decades. In 1963, Dylan wrote "Only a Pawn in their Game" about the murder of Medgar Evers, and "The Lonesome Death of Hattie Carroll," about the murder of a black 51-year-old woman by a wealthy young man who received only a six-month jail sentence for the crime. Bob Dylan also appeared at a number of civil rights rallies, including the historic March on Washington. Although some commentators have faulted him for abandoning his civil rights commitment later in his career, Dylan has regularly returned to racial issues in his work. Among the most notable was his 1975 song about wrongly imprisoned boxer Rubin Carter, titled "Hurricane."

Dylan's contemporary, Phil Ochs (1940–1976), likewise wrote and performed classic songs that became staples of the civil rights movement. He also appeared at many civil rights rallies, singing songs to bolster the enthusiasm of activists. Among his many topical songs, "Talking Birmingham Jam," "Here's to the State of Mississippi," and "Too Many Martyrs" all dealt specifically with issues relevant to the racial times of the 1960s. Ochs's untimely suicide in 1976 deprived admirers of additional musical creations, but his legacy as a major cultural figure of his time remains secure.

Phil Ochs

Many other musical artists made vital contributions to the civil rights movement. Joan Baez, Nina Simone, Gil Scott-Heron, and John Coltrane all participated, sang, and wrote lyrics about the struggles of African Americans and their supporters. Though younger than others with direct experience in 60s activities, Bruce Springsteen has kept the musical momentum alive by regularly singing the iconic anthems of the movement, offering contemporary audiences a glimpse of the emotional energy and inspiration that they provided so effectively.

Bruce Springsteen

LITERATURE

Literary artists had a profound influence on the cause as well. Like their musician counterparts, many writers felt politically engaged and saw their works as integral components of the struggle. Novels, essays, plays, and poems may have lacked the immediate emotional impact of music but still resonated powerfully with civil rights advocates. Moreover, literary efforts retained important historical value in reminding younger generations of the efforts of the past.

Langston Hughes

African American writers have focused on race, racial identity, and the struggle for freedom and equality for centuries. They have created a vast body of literature that now constitutes a respected academic specialty in colleges and universities throughout the world. The variety of African American literature tradition is vast and growing, ranging from slave narratives and other autobiographies to spiritual quests, depictions of urban and rural black life, protest works, and much more.

Zora Neal Hurstont

The Harlem Renaissance marked a high point during the 1920s and 1930s, when African American writers richly chronicled multiple dimensions of the black experience. Authors like Langston Hughes, Zora Neale Hurston, Jean Toomer, Countee Cullen, and others brought African American themes to larger audiences, including readers outside the black community. Later, luminaries like Richard Wright, Lorraine Hansberry, Ralph Ellison, and several others continued the distinguished tradition of African American literary achievement. All of these figures influenced in various ways the writers most strongly associated with the civil rights and Black Power era.

The dramatic events of those times encouraged many writers, predominantly black, to use their literary talents to respond to the contemporary ferment. Deeply affected by the new militancy on the streets, they expressed their own feelings and support in their novels, short stories, essays, poems, and other genres. Their approaches varied and often expressed major theoretical and ideological differences.

Jean Toomer

Countee Cullen

One of the writers most closely associated with the modern civil rights movement was James Baldwin (1924–1987). Widely recognized as the major literary voice calling attention to American racism in the early and mid-1960s, Baldwin had already created a distinguished body of literature and had lived extensively in France. From the late 1950s, however, he returned to America and became deeply involved in the civil rights struggle. He made a prominent appearance at the March on Washington and traveled to Selma, Alabama, to lend his support to the civil rights campaign, later joining the historic march from there to Montgomery. He spoke regularly about civil rights, gaining high national and international visibility for his efforts.

James Baldwin

Baldwin's essays were his primary medium to express his views about racial issues in America. His *Notes of a Native Son* (1955) and *Nobody Knows My Name: More Notes of a Native Son* (1961) contained several essays addressing the racial crisis in America. In 1963, Baldwin wrote *The Fire Next Time*, one of the most powerful and widely read statements about race and a trenchant critique of religion. Among frontline participants, it was virtually impossible to find anyone unfamiliar with this work. Baldwin's book was blunt in its warning to the majority white population: "The brutality with which Negroes are treated in this country simply cannot be overstated, however unwilling white men may be to hear it." His candor landed him on the cover of *Time* Magazine for his brutally perceptive vision of the racial revolution sweeping the nation.

In 1964, Baldwin wrote a play titled *Blues for Mister Charlie*, based on the murder of Emmett Till. A year later he collaborated with photographer

Richard Avedon on *Nothing Personal*, contributing an essay intended as a tribute to Medgar Evers. Even after the civil rights era, he continued his productivity until his death, remaining a perceptive and critical observer of race relations in America.

Just as James Baldwin was inextricably linked to the civil rights movement, LeRoi Jones (later Amiri Baraka, 1934–2014) is associated with the Black Power and Black Arts movements. A poet, playwright, novelist, and public intellectual, Baraka expressed decades of black anger and used the written word as a powerful weapon against American racism. Baraka underwent many ideological transformations over the years, but his plays, essays, music criticism, and political commentaries made him one of the most prominent African American literary figures of the 20th and early 21st centuries.

/LeRoi Jones/ Amiri Baraka

Baraka had a close connection with the black nationalist tradition and has influenced numerous other writers and cultural activists. He has empowered African American readers to revel in their own racial identity and has pushed white Americans to confront the reality of their own racist impulses and attitudes. He was a cultural and literary force not easily ignored beginning in the mid-1960s, and his literary and political efforts during the most turbulent times of racial unrest made him one of the most controversial African American figures of the modern era.

Baraka moved to Harlem in 1965 and established the Black Arts Repertory Theater, which marked the beginning of the Black Arts Movement. His 1966 poem "Black Art" reflected the growing militancy of its adherents and armed self-defense as a focus of the era. With provocative language—such as "we want poems that kill"—Baraka echoed the strong rhetoric of the era. At the same time, that poem and some subsequent writings and public statements contained some ill-chosen language about Jews that dogged him throughout his career and diminished his impact on the wider community supportive of racial justice in America.

Baraka's earlier plays like *The Dutchman* and his musical criticism like *Blues People* had established him as a major African American literary voice, making his move from the integrationist, nonviolent civil rights movement extremely noticeable. In 1967, he established a close relationship with Maulana Karenga and became a key advocate of Karenga's vision of Kawaida. As Professor Scot Brown notes, for Baraka this meant to expose the enemy, praise the people, and support the revolution. His poem "Who Will Survive America/Few Americans/Very Few Negroes/No crackers at all" was the quintessential literary vision of black cultural nationalism, widely read and appreciated in those circles. In 1968, Baraka and his colleague Larry Neal published *Black Fire: An Anthology of Afro-American Writing*, an excellent source book of almost 200 writings reflecting the political and cultural ferment of that era.

Amiri Baraka subsequently became a Marxist, moving away from his earlier political and literary posture. But he continued to write prolifically and to generate controversy in his written works and public statements. Like that of James Baldwin, his influence on his contemporaries and younger colleagues has been profound.

Gwendolyn Brooks

Many other literary figures, including several women, are likewise closely associated with the modern black freedom struggles. Gwendolyn Brooks (1917–2000) was the first African American to win a Pulitzer Prize for poetry, in 1950. During the Black Power phase of the civil rights crusade, her poetry became more socially oriented and she was associated with the Black Arts Movement. Like many of her contemporaries, Brooks wrote primarily about black issues for black audiences.

125

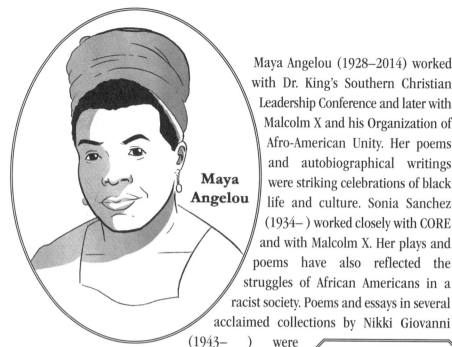

Maya Angelou

Maya Angelou (1928–2014) worked with Dr. King's Southern Christian Leadership Conference and later with Malcolm X and his Organization of Afro-American Unity. Her poems and autobiographical writings were striking celebrations of black life and culture. Sonia Sanchez (1934–) worked closely with CORE and with Malcolm X. Her plays and poems have also reflected the struggles of African Americans in a racist society. Poems and essays in several acclaimed collections by Nikki Giovanni (1943–) were similarly inspired by the civil rights and Black Power movement of the 60s and early 70s.

Dudley Randall (1914–2000), a Detroit-based publisher and poet, used his position to publish the works of many talented African American contemporaries. As a poet, Randall's own "Ballad of Birmingham" is a haunting reminder of the horrific 1963 church bombing that killed four young girls. Ed Bullins (1935–), another key figure of the Black Arts Movement, worked with the Black Panther Party

Dudley Randall

and eventually became Minister of Culture for that militant organization. His plays dealt with the black experience and reflected the difficulties of life for working-class blacks.

Ed Bullins

All of these writers and their many colleagues added a significant dimension to the political struggles of their people. If their creative products were not always available on the front lines of confrontation, they were widely read in African American political settings at the time. Equally important, their works even now reveal the passion and fervor of the times and suggest disconcertingly that many of the goals of that era remain unfilled into the 21ˢᵗ century.

VISUAL ARTS

Visual artists played a unique if no less vital role in the modern civil rights movement. Probably the most visible contributions were the posters, banners, and buttons that were integral to demonstrations, rallies, and meetings. Foot soldiers of the movement with graphic design talent produced many or most of these materials. Although their authorship remained largely anonymous, they added a vibrant emotional element to the activism of the era.

Many prominent professional artists also made striking contributions, many of which have added to the ever-increasing stature of the African American artistic tradition. They continued a major current of African American art history found in such predecessors as Edmonia Lewis, Aaron Douglas, Claude Clarke, Hale Woodruff, Lois Mailou Jones, Cliff Joseph, Jacob Lawrence, John Biggers, and scores of others. These gifted artists regularly addressed racial justice issues in their work. Understandably, black visual artists have always been committed to the struggles of their people and, like their musical and literary counterparts, they saw their art as serious contributions to these historic battles.

One of the key figures was Elizabeth Catlett (1915–2012), the exemplar of a socially engaged artist. A sculptor and printmaker, Catlett regularly made portraits of historical luminaries, such as Sojourner Truth,

Elizabeth Catlett

Harriet Tubman, and Angela Davis. Her prints provided striking support for historic African American struggles for freedom and dignity. Prints such as "Civil Rights Congress" (1949) and "Malcolm Speaks for Us" (1969) reveal her abiding commitment to the cause. Sculptures such as "Homage to My Young Black Sisters" (1968), "Black Unity" (1968), and "Target" (1970) were well known among activists and serve as a strong reminder of the tradition of militant black protest.

Charles White

Charles White (1918–1979) also used his prodigious visual talent to communicate his social perspective, which included a strong vision of black liberation. Above all, he depicted images of African American dignity, in dramatic contrast to the stereotypical portrayals of his people that dominated popular culture even through the modern civil rights era. His portraits of major historical figures like Harriet Tubman, W.E.B. Du Bois, Paul Robeson, and others were also well known among liberation activists during that time.

One of the most active artists of the movement was Faith Ringgold (1930–), who has spent a lifetime as an activist/artist fighting for her fellow African Americans and for women. Her paintings, quilts, and children's books are full of strong imagery that calls attention to American racism and sexism. Ringgold has played a vigorous role in various feminist and anti-racist organizations and has shown that artistic excellence and personal activism are mutually enhancing—a lesson with a strong impact on younger, socially committed artists from the modern civil rights era to the present.

Faith Ringgold

David Hammons (1943–) produced several provocative works during his younger years in Los Angeles. In 1969, for example, he created a three-dimensional piece titled "Door," which showed an admissions office barring African Americans from entry—an issue that propelled many students to work to remedy racial discrimination in American education. In 1970, Hammons produced a print titled "Injustice Case," a stark commentary about Black Panther leader Bobby Seale when Judge Julius Hoffman bound and gagged him in the courtroom during the trial of the Chicago Seven.

David Hammons

These works found widely enthusiastic audiences within the movement.

Massachusetts native Dana Chandler (1941–) has been an artistic provocateur throughout his career. His visual works reflect the tradition of black protest and activism, condemning KKK crimes against women and the emasculation and incarceration of black men, while presenting positive images of black figures such as Medgar Evers, Martin Luther King, Muhammad Ali, and Nelson Mandela. His pieces have contributed vigorously to the robust civil rights activity of the Boston area where he lives and works.

Dana Chandler

The official artist of the Black Panther Party was Emory Douglas (1943–), whose works were probably the best known and most accessible of the Black Power era. A prolific and talented graphic agitator, he produced hundreds of works

Emory Douglas

129

for the party's newspaper, *The Black Panther*, which had a circulation of well over 100,000. Douglas's savage caricatures of racist white politicians and police officers and his portraits of strong African American women, men, and children resisting oppression are landmarks of visual social commentary. His posters about police harassment and deplorable housing conditions were plastered throughout black neighborhoods, inviting ordinary blacks to rise up in protest, with armed force if necessary.

In addition to these individual artists (and many others), community muralists, often working in collaborative teams with younger artists and teenage apprentices, added a colorful public art dimension to the civil rights movement. Their works encouraged people to see outstanding artwork with provocative political content in the course of their daily lives, reinforcing their commitment to social action. The United States had many politically oriented murals during the WPA days of the Depression. Earlier black artists like Hale Woodruff and Charles White created major mural works in the late 1930s and early 1940s respectively that commemorated African American struggles of that era.

William Walker

The 1960s mural renaissance was concentrated in urban areas with large minority populations. The murals that emerged typically expressed themes that reflected the racial conflicts on the nation's streets. And they appeared across the country. In Chicago, black artists William Walker (1927–2011), Jeff Donaldson (1932–2004), Eugene Eda (1939–), and others spearheaded the mural movement, bringing the civil rights movement to the streets with

Jeff Donaldson

colorful, pulsating energy. White muralists Mark Rogovin (1945–) and John Pitman Weber (1942–) added their own efforts to the tradition, working closely with African American youth in bringing civil rights messages to minority communities. Joe Stephenson in New York, Dana Chandler in Boston, Dewey Crumpler (1949–) in San Francisco, John Feagin in Montgomery, and Elliot Pinkney (1934–) and Charles Freeman (1951–) in Los Angeles, among others throughout the nation, also painted murals about American civil rights struggles. In Los Angeles, Noni Olabisi continued the tradition in 1996 by producing a controversial mural praising the Black Panther Party ("To Protect and Serve").

James Van der Zee

Finally, photographers have played a huge role in disseminating visual information about civil rights activities for several generations. One of the earliest examples was James Van der Zee's (1886–1983) documentation of Marcus Garvey and the Universal Negro Improvement Association in Harlem. Twins Morgan Smith (1910–1993) and Marvin Smith (1910–2003) documented Adam Clayton Powell leading civil rights demonstrations in Harlem in the early 1940s and anti-lynching demonstrations in New York during the same period. Gordon Parks (1912–2006), one of America's most broadly accomplished artists, photographed Southern segregation and, later in his career, Malcolm X and Black Panther Party leaders and members.

Gordon Parks

Several photojournalists documented the modern civil rights movement of the 1950s and 1960s. Moneta Sleet (1926–1996), Jack Franklin (1922–2009), and Ernest Withers (1922–2007) all addressed issues of racial violence, the organizing efforts of civil rights workers, marches, rallies, and demonstrations, and related themes. Jonathan Eubanks (1927–) became known for his photographs of the Black Panther Party, providing a comprehensive vision of its political and community service activities. Robert Haggins (1922–2006) was the personal photographer of Malcolm X, providing a glimpse into the personal and public dimensions of his extraordinary life.

FILM

A powerful medium of cultural expression, film has effectively brought the civil rights movement to audiences of millions throughout the nation and the world. Unlike music, literature, and the visual arts, most civil rights films have been produced *after* the actual events. Their primary value is historical and educational; they provide a cinematic record and interpretation of what happened. They frequently arouse strong audience emotions and often intentionally promote the will to continue civil rights activities in the present and future.

Both documentary and feature films offer viewers a glimpse of some of the most dramatic historical events in American civil rights history. Documentary films usually employ actual footage and narratives, often from movement participants and sympathetic scholars and other commentators. Although popular opinion often perceives documentary films as "objective" accounts of historical happenings, they are, in fact, reflections of the values and biases of the directors who create them. They have clear points of view, and most civil rights documentaries reflect the aims and objectives of the protestors they depict.

The 14-hour documentary series *Eyes on the Prize* (1987–1990) is generally considered the most comprehensive, landmark account of the entire modern civil rights movement, from the *Brown* decision and Emmett Till murder to the black nationalist and Black Power activities and the affirmative action controversies of later decades. The segments also include virtually all of the major episodes chronicled in earlier chapters of this volume. Created and produced by Henry Hampton at Blackside, the series

Henry Hampton

Julian Bond

skillfully weaves together archival footage and interviews from the major players from 1954 to 1985, including civil rights activists and recalcitrant Southern racists.

Each segment runs approximately one-hour and is eloquently narrated by Julian Bond, whose civil rights record of more than a half century makes him one of the most respected figures of the movement. The most striking feature of *Eyes on the Prize* is its treatment of the ordinary African Americans and their supporters from other races who put their lives on the line for dignity and the legal and moral rights they deserved. The series is an indispensable source for scholars and laypersons alike.

Most other documentaries focus on specific civil rights events or historical figures. *King: A Filmed Record from Montgomery to Memphis* (1970) chronicles the short and dynamic political life of Martin Luther King, using archival footage from his speeches, demonstrations, and arrests and images of police repression. With celebrity appearances by Harry Belafonte, James Earl Jones, Paul Newman, Burt Lancaster, Ruby Dee, and others, this three-hour documentary provides an invaluable record of King's remarkable legacy as one of the greatest figures in U.S. history.

Nelson Stanley

Stanley Nelson's 2010 *Freedom Riders* gives viewers the stories of the hundreds of black and white men and women who braved Southern mob and police violence and brutal jail conditions to end segregation in interstate travel. Its focus on the human dimension fulfills the finest function of socially conscious art by encouraging both intellectual reflection and emotional reaction. *Mighty Times: The Children's March*, a short documentary that the Southern Poverty Law Center co-produced in 2004, focuses on the Birmingham events of 1963 and the remarkable role of African American children in that crusade.

Negroes With Guns: Rob Williams and Black Power, by Sandra Dickson, is a 2005 documentary film that provides a fuller, more sympathetic portrait of this major Black Power figure. The film reveals why Williams decided to arm the members of the African American community in Monroe, North Carolina.

With a skillful combination of footage and interviews, this documentary provides the comprehensive backstory about Klan violence and legal racism in Monroe, leading to Williams's view that he had no choice other than armed self-defense. *Negroes With Guns* goes a long way in restoring Williams to his rightful place in the history of African American liberation struggles.

Spike Lee is universally regarded as one of the premier contemporary African American filmmakers. His exemplary documentaries and

Spike Lee

feature films about race in America have set the qualitative standard for the medium. His 1997 documentary *4 Little Girls* focuses on the horrific 1963 Birmingham church bombing that killed four young girls a few weeks after the March on Washington. Lee's portrait of the girls offers a deeply personal vision, including the devastating impact on their families. In the process, he uses film to reveal how the civil rights movement was much more than an abstract social phenomenon: it was a crusade that affected real people, often for the good but sometimes tragically.

Feature films with civil rights themes have likewise affected large American audiences. As in the case of documentaries, there have been a myriad of influential releases. *The Long Walk Home* (1990), directed by Richard Pearce, dramatizes the Montgomery bus boycott of 1955–1956 and focuses on the actions and emotions of black and white women during that historic battle. A key element of the film involves the role of the white female protagonist, who provides transportation for her African American domestic worker, played by Whoopi Goldberg. After severe pressure from her husband and other racist whites, she joins the carpool system that allowed blacks to continue their successful boycott. The film mirrors actual events during those turbulent times and shows that some white women actually came to understand the plight of their domestic employees.

Racist murders in Mississippi generated two dramatic feature films with different perspectives. *Mississippi Burning,* directed by Alan Parker, was a 1988 thriller based loosely on the 1964 murders of SNCC workers James Chaney, Andrew Goodman, and Mickey Schwerner. At once engaging and informative, the film effectively depicts the small-town racial hatred that led to the murders and the resulting national outcry. At the same time, many civil rights insiders were highly critical of the film's overly sympathetic portray of the FBI, in contrast to the actual indifference and even hostility of that agency towards civil rights workers during much of the modern civil rights movement.

Rob Reiner's *Ghosts of Mississippi* (1996) dramatizes the aftermath of the Medgar Evers's 1963 murder. The storyline focuses on Evers's widow Myrlie Evers's protracted attempt to bring murderer Byron De La Beckwith to justice. Her quest, with the help of a sympathetic white prosecutor, was ultimately successful, as De La Beckwith was convicted and sentenced to life imprisonment—three decades after the crime.

One of Spike Lee's most ambitious feature films was his biopic of Malcolm X in 1992. *Malcolm X,* with Denzel Washington in the title role, recounts Malcolm's entire life, from his boyhood in Nebraska and his youthful criminal years in Massachusetts to his imprisonment, relationship and rupture with the Nation of Islam, pilgrimage to Mecca, and assassination. The film starts provocatively with actual footage of the Los Angeles Police Department beating of Rodney King in 1992, linking Malcolm's story with contemporary racial events that swept America into a frenzy following the not-guilty verdict for King's assailants. As much as Alex Haley's *Autobiography of Malcolm X* in 1965, Lee's film restored Malcolm to mainstream public consideration and elevated him as one of the most iconic figures in the long struggle for African American liberation.

Two made-for-television films, with less exposure than blockbuster Hollywood productions, nevertheless added a valuable dimension to the body of civil rights films. *The Ernest Green Story* (1993) was a biopic about the only senior-class member of the courageous Little Rock students who braved racist mobs and defiant Arkansas Governor Orval Faubus in 1957. Filmed on location at Central High School, it featured major African American film stars Ossie Davis, Ruby Dee, C.C.H. Pounder, and others. Characteristic of the genre, the film focused on the human dimensions of the subject and his fellow students, with the background events serving as wider context. *Deacons for Defense,* which aired on cable TV in 2003, told the story of the Louisiana men who formed an armed guard to patrol their communities and defend themselves against

Ernest Green

white racist violence. The film brought the Deacons into national prominence and encouraged viewers to understand them in the broader context of the Black Power movement of the times.

In 2013, director Steve McQueen presented *12 Years A Slave,* the story of Solomon Northup who was kidnapped and enslaved in the early 19th century. Large audiences saw the horrors of slavery in this film. These brutalities catalyzed the abolitionist and other resistance movements described in earlier chapters in the book. The film won the Academy Award for best Picture in 2014. *Selma*, directed by Ava DuVernay, was also a major feature film from 2014. It focused on Dr. Martin Luther king and his civil rights colleagues during the campaign in 1963 for voting rights. Its most dramatic scenes treated the historic march from Selma, Alabama to Montgomery, Alabama and brought dramatic attention to the brutality of Southern police against nonviolent civil rights protestors.

Cultural expressions in all forms have made monumental contributions to the continuing campaigns for racial justice. Singers, songwriters, novelists, playwrights, poets, essayists, visual artists, and filmmakers all have used their prodigious talents to criticize the inequities of social and political life and to offer visions for social change and transformation. That process continues in the early 21st century, adding great distinction to national artistic life.

Chapter 7:

THE INFLUENCE OF THE CIVIL RIGHTS MOVEMENT: OTHER LIBERATION MOVEMENTS FROM THE 1960S TO THE PRESENT

The modern civil rights movement, which lasted from the mid-1950s through much of the 1970s, was the dominant protest movement of an entire era dominated by social and political unrest. At the same time, its high visibility and profound moral vision encouraged many other groups with longstanding histories of oppression and legitimate grievances to emulate and adapt to their own needs the movement's organizational structures, its capacity for mass mobilization, and even its strategies and tactics. The civil rights movement set the tone for one of the most tumultuous political times in modern American history.

THE STUDENT AND ANTIWAR MOVEMENTS

One of the most immediate developments emerging from the nonviolent phase of the civil rights movement occurred at the University of California campus in Berkeley during the fall of 1964. Berkeley had long been a center of radical political activism. In 1963 and 1964, the San Francisco Bay Area was the site of numerous civil rights demonstrations, with the vigorous participation of Berkeley students. Campus authorities took steps to restrict the recruitment of Berkeley students after large numbers used the campus to demonstrate at the Republican Convention in San Francisco in July 1964 and at the *Oakland Tribune* newspaper, owned by conservative former Republican Senator William Knowland, throughout that summer.

University officials decreed that students could no longer use university property to recruit for off-campus political activity—a policy directed specifically against civil rights activism. Many students resisted immediately, seeing the decree as an egregious violation of their First Amendment rights and as an attempt to squelch their efforts to resist the continuing racial discrimination of many local employers. Among those who took part in the Free Speech Movement (FSM) were hundreds who had had extensive frontline experience in the civil rights movement, including efforts in the Deep South with SNCC and other groups. The most charismatic leader of the FSM was Mario Savio, who had returned from Freedom Summer in Mississippi for his undergraduate studies at Berkeley. It was a common refrain among FSM activists, often with sarcasm, that they had already encountered violent Southern sheriffs and the Ku Klux Klan and that university deans and bureaucrats were hardly likely to induce much fear and apprehension.

During the fall semester of 1964, demonstrations grew and confrontations intensified. In December, almost 800 persons, mostly students, were arrested in an occupation of the university administration

Mario Savio

building that resulted in a mass civil disobedience action. In a famous speech before the sit-in, Savio declared, "you've got to put your bodies upon the gears and upon the wheels, upon the levers, upon all the apparatus, and you've got to make it stop." This dramatic protest, following the classic model of the civil rights movement, convinced the Berkeley faculty to support the FSM, granting student activists considerable political rights that they used for decades to come. The FSM was the model of campus protests until violent confrontations broke out over the Vietnam War in the late 1960s and early 1970s.

The second half of the 1960s, with the escalation of the war in Vietnam, saw the emergence of a growing antiwar movement. As with the FSM, the increasing fervor of domestic opposition to U.S. military involvement in Vietnam and throughout Southeast Asia built on the energy of the civil rights protests. Students were the heart and soul of the antiwar movement, drawing on their experiences in civil rights and various campus crusades. Major "teach-ins" at the University of Michigan in 1965 and soon afterwards at the University of California at Berkeley catalyzed local and national protests against the war.

Resistance grew significantly when major elements of the civil rights movement joined the antiwar effort. SNCC activists including Robert Moses, James Foreman, and others had opposed U.S. policy in Vietnam from the outset. In 1965, the organization issued a detailed position paper against the war.

A critical moment occurred on April 4, 1967, when the Rev. Martin Luther King spoke passionately at the Riverside Church in New York City, where he declared his profound moral opposition to the Vietnam War. His speech, reminiscent of his earlier "Letter from the Birmingham Jail," criticized a nation that sent black men to fight and die in Vietnam but refused to give them jobs and justice at home. King received rebukes from members of the African American community, including some in the civil rights movement, for his courageous stand. They felt that he was deflecting attention from the continuing efforts against racism. But King's moral courage prevailed, encouraging many in the civil rights community to recognize that President Lyndon Johnson's ill-conceived war effort was deflecting resources from urgent domestic priorities and that young black and brown men were dying disproportionately in a fight against other people of color.

Nonviolent resistance to the war, including civil disobedience, intensified as demonstrators adopted the strategies and tactics of the earlier civil rights organizations. The idealism and courage of the civil rights movement were replicated throughout the country. By the late 1960s, the Vietnam War had polarized the United States, and opposition to it eventually became the majority view as the fighting slogged on to its inglorious conclusion.

THE CHICANO MOVEMENT

African Americans were only one minority group to organize politically for their civil rights. Their historic campaign inspired other people of color to mobilize for recognition of cultural heritage, equal economic and political opportunity, and an end to discrimination in the criminal justice system. The Mexican American/Chicano community, in particular, stepped up its long, hard fight against racial discrimination and for civil rights.

Chicano activist Cesar Chavez is one of America's best-known labor leaders, whose commitment to the struggle for equality and legacy of nonviolent action is comparable to that of Martin Luther King. Like King, Chavez would be the first to note that he was only one of many Chicano activists. Among his immediate forerunners was Ernesto Galarza, who organized Mexican American farmworkers in California in the years after World War II. Although he achieved only limited success, Galarza's work in the 1940s and 1950s set the stage for more effective efforts in the following decade.

In the 1960s, low wages and deplorable working conditions made life miserable for thousands of Chicano farmworkers and their families, especially in California's fertile Central Valley. In 1960, Dolores Huerta founded the Agricultural Workers Organizing Committee (AWOC), and two years later, she accepted Chavez's invitation to work with him in creating a full-fledged farmworkers' union. The new organization commenced strikes and boycotts in order to negotiate fair working agreements with growers.

Cesar Chavez

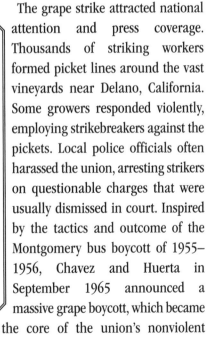

Dolores Huerta

The grape strike attracted national attention and press coverage. Thousands of striking workers formed picket lines around the vast vineyards near Delano, California. Some growers responded violently, employing strikebreakers against the pickets. Local police officials often harassed the union, arresting strikers on questionable charges that were usually dismissed in court. Inspired by the tactics and outcome of the Montgomery bus boycott of 1955–1956, Chavez and Huerta in September 1965 announced a massive grape boycott, which became the core of the union's nonviolent strategy. In 1966, the unions merged, forming the United Farm Workers Union (UFW), eventually winning passage of the nation's first farm labor act in California and reaching agreement with most growers in the Central Valley.

Reies Tijerina

Other groups also played major roles in the Chicano civil rights struggles. In 1967, a young leader named Reies Tijerina led a group of 350 protestors in occupying federal land in a New Mexico forest. This group, called *aliancistas*, claimed the land under the 1848 Treaty of Guadalupe Hidalgo, which ended the Mexican-American War. Tijerina's dramatic actions took their cue from Mexican history, particularly the protests of revolutionary leader Emiliano Zapata in the 1910s. Later in 1967, Tijerina led a raid on a New Mexico courthouse, seeking to recover land he believed was improperly distributed after New Mexico's annexation by the United States. Tijerina and several supporters were arrested and jailed. After his release, Tijerina allied himself with militant African American and Native American organizations. He is regarded as a major symbol of militant Chicano activism.

Throughout the American Southwest, other Chicano civil rights organizations appeared, including Crusade for Justice in Colorado and La Raza Unida in Texas. Los Angeles, with its huge Latino population, was also a longtime center for Chicano activism. In 1968, at the height of American civil rights ferment, 10,000 Chicano students and several teachers in Los Angeles high schools organized a walkout. They protested the quality of public education and sought recognition of their cultural heritage. Chicano activists picketed the Los Angeles School Board, held sit-ins, teach-ins, and rallies. A major group supporting the school walkout was the Brown Berets, a Chicano equivalent of the Black Panthers.

In 1970, hundreds of thousands of Los Angeles residents marched in the Chicano Moratorium. This was a peaceful demonstration against the Vietnam War, protesting the disproportionate number of Mexican American casualties in that conflict. Los Angeles police used tear gas and clubs to disperse the demonstration, reminiscent of Southern police repression. Chicano resistance has continued in the decades since, supporting affirmative action, immigration reform, an end to police harassment, and other issues deeply relevant to that growing community.

THE AMERICAN INDIAN MOVEMENT

Dennis Banks

Russell Means

In similar fashion, the civil rights movement also encouraged American Indians to organize around their discontent over horrific mistreatment through history and ongoing neglect in American society. The American Indian Movement (AIM) was founded in 1968 in Minneapolis, reflecting a vision of "Red Power" that emulated the Black Power focus of that era. Its most prominent early leaders were Dennis Banks and Russell Means. Like other civil rights organizations, AIM addressed poverty, urban blight, and police misconduct and harassment. Unique to its mission, it also focused on the unsavory history of broken government treaties with Native American peoples.

The organization's most dramatic early action occurred in fall 1969, when hundreds of American Indians occupied the abandoned prison site of Alcatraz Island in San Francisco Bay. The protestors demanded the deed for the island and called for the creation of a Native American museum, university, and cultural center. The occupation attracted massive media attention and lasted until June 1971. It dramatized the desperate and deplorable conditions of American Indians, whose plight had been ignored by mainstream America. Student activists, Indians from reservations, and urban residents all joined in the action and remained on the island until their removal by federal marshals.

AIM continued its militant actions after Alcatraz. In 1972, it sponsored a march on Washington called the Trail of Broken Treaties and briefly occupied the federal Bureau of Indian Affairs office. The organization issued a list of demands to President Richard Nixon, who was unsympathetic. Following the militant example of its African American allies, AIM in February 1973 occupied the town Wounded Knee, South Dakota, on the Pine Ridge Indian Reservation. Wounded Knee was the site of the historic Indian armed resistance against U.S. forces in 1890 that resulted in the massacre of hundreds of Indian men, women, and children.

The Wounded Knee protest also garnered massive media coverage. The siege lasted 71 days and involved armed Indians against U.S. government forces. Many people were wounded, resulting in wholesale arrests and indictments. But the confrontation brought international visibility to their plight, finally making American Indian issues a serious item on the national political agenda. Like African American and Chicano activists, native peoples have continued their struggle to remedy the enormous social and economic barriers they still face in American society. Their high unemployment, lack of access to health care and other social services, and inadequate educational resources on reservations and elsewhere continue to keep them marginalized. Protests against stereotypical and degrading use of Indian figures, symbols, and mascots in collegiate and professional sports have also mobilized the American Indian civil rights community. Native American civil rights activism is far from finished in the early 21st century.

THE ASIAN AMERICAN MOVEMENT

Asian Americans also mobilized to seek redress for a host of grievances in the wake of the civil rights actions by people of color. Often stereotyped as the "model minority," Asian Americans from a multitude of national backgrounds have mistakenly been viewed as passive and averse to conflict and confrontation. Like other ethnic and civil rights struggles, the Asian American movement mobilized consciousness within several national communities and brought wider public attention to issues that had been ignored in public discourse and debate. Demands for "Yellow Power" joined the multicultural chorus of activism sweeping the nation in the 1960s.

The manifestation of Asian American civil rights activism also emerged from a longer historical tradition. Chinese Americans had often resisted egregious discrimination and racism, especially in Pacific Coast states. Japanese Americans had protested the disgraceful incarceration of more than 110,000 persons of Japanese ancestry from California, Oregon, and Washington in American concentration camps under Executive Order 9066 in 1942, after Pearl Harbor. In the 1960s, a younger generation of Japanese American activists, influenced by civil rights movement gains, started the "Redress Movement," demanding an official apology for the "internment" of 1942–1945. They finally received an apology from President Gerald Ford in 1976, but the Japanese American Citizens League pressed the issue further and in 1988 finally gained reparation payments of $20,000 for each living detainee of the camps.

Filipino Americans contributed their own history of activism to this legacy. Under the leadership of Larry Itliong, for example, they played a significant role in agricultural labor organizing in California during the 1960s. In 1956, Itliong organized the Filipino Farm Labor Union and later joined with Cesar Chavez and Dolores Huerta in organizing the Delano grape strike of 1965. Filipino farmworkers joined their Chicano colleagues in fighting against the inhumane working conditions, unfair treatment, and low wages that dominated the agricultural workplace at the time.

Larry Itliong

By the early 1970s, young Asian Americans had formed activist groups at numerous colleges and universities. They acknowledged that the "black is beautiful" vision of African Americans generated pride in their own ethnic heritages. That consciousness encouraged them to combat the stereotypical notions of passivity and accommodation to white domination. They were

Vincent Chin

instrumental in multiracial coalitions to create ethnic studies programs at various educational levels. More recently, Asian American protest has targeted racial violence, including the infamous 1982 Vincent Chin murder in Detroit, the exploitation of immigrant Asians, especially women, in U.S. sweatshops and other workplaces, and the stereotypical and sexualized depictions of Asians in entertainment and the media.

THE FEMINIST MOVEMENT

The American feminist movement, with its long and proud historical roots, emerged even more vigorously in the wake of the black freedom movement. Some of the impetus occurred as a result of sexism within the civil rights movement itself, a reality that cannot and should not be ignored. SNCC was forced to address the issue when a group of women demanded that the organization confront its sexual discrimination. Staff members Casey Hayden and Mary King wrote in 1965 that women were routinely asked to perform trivial office tasks and prevented from major policy roles and decision-making authority. Their paper compared the plight of women to that of blacks in general, with a similar pattern of subordination and diminished respect.

Casey Hayden

Mary King

Many male civil rights leaders ignored such

complaints, seeing the racial struggle as significantly more serious. Stokely Carmichael, responding to a question about the proper role of women in SNCC, replied "prone." The comment was widely condemned in feminist circles. The Black Panther Party, despite its formal condemnation of sexism and commitment to gender equality, also had a legacy of sexism within its structure and operations. Women played a large role in its history, to be sure, but male members and their patriarchal views often dominated when political decisions were made and implemented. Too many male Panthers believed that women's roles were primarily to nurture the men who would truly bring forth the black revolution.

Many disaffected women from the black struggle became major feminist activists of the 1960s and 1970s. The women's liberation movement, with mostly young white women, was also nurtured in the political, social, and cultural environments of the civil rights and other protest movements. Like other women activists of the era, they followed in the path of the long struggle of women for full equality in the United States. They discovered the proud history of their predecessors, learning about women's activism in the labor movement, the fight for birth control and reproductive freedom, and above all, the heroic suffragists who fought for decades for the right to vote, not granted until the 19th Amendment was finally ratified in 1920. They began to adapt the efforts and tactics of historical feminists to the pressing needs of the present, focusing on abortion, sexual politics (with the perceptive slogan "the personal is political"), workplace equity and job discrimination, day care, sexual violence, increased educational and professional opportunities, and other gender issues.

Throughout the modern civil rights era, women's liberation groups employed many familiar tactics. In 1968 at the Miss America Pageant in Atlantic City, New Jersey, feminist protestors tossed pots, pans, false eyelashes, and other items to condemn the treatment of women as little more than sexual body parts for the voyeuristic pleasure of men. The demonstration drew large media coverage and brought the women's movement to international attention. The movement continued by agitating to abolish abortion laws, culminating in the 1973 U.S. Supreme Court decision in *Roe v. Wade*, which made reproductive choice a part of the constitutional right to privacy.

Women (and some male supporters) also used activism against corporations guilty of gender discrimination, demanded and achieved job gains in the military and in sports, created rape crisis centers and battered women's shelters, and effected changes in divorce and inheritance laws that discriminated against women's property rights. The women's liberation movement also played a major role in creating women's studies programs throughout American higher education, increased female participation among elected officials, and reduced (but hardly eliminated) repulsive images of women in advertising and other media. Those goals and others continue as part of a younger generation of feminist activists.

THE GAY LIBERATION MOVEMENT

Lesbian, gay, bisexual, and transgender (LGBT) Americans have been among the most vocal and effective in following the footsteps of the civil rights movement. During the 1960s and 70s, gay issues were scarcely on the national agenda. Hostility toward homosexuals was rampant, even in movements dedicated to other aspects of human liberation. In the civil rights movement, for example, Bayard Rustin, an openly gay African American man, was covertly and sometimes overtly attacked for his sexual orientation despite his brilliant capacity for organizing.

In the late 1960s, gay men and women began their modern movement for equal treatment, to eliminate violence and discrimination, and to instill pride and dignity in their own community. Like women liberationists, they

Bayard Rustin

150

Harry
Hay

discovered the historical roots of their social activism. The major figure was Harry Hay (1912–2002), a longtime activist with trade unions, the Communist Party, and an organization he founded in 1950 called the Mattachine Society. Highly secret, the organization was dedicated to protecting the homosexual minority. A major issue was police harassment and entrapment, which often ruined the lives of men charged with sexual offenses. The Mattachine Society started in Los Angeles and established chapters in San Francisco, Chicago, New York, and Washington, D.C. The Daughters of Bilitis was the counterpart lesbian organization, and the two groups worked together on issues of mutual concern. Above all, both organizations enabled gay people to develop a self-loving identity and to break down the self-loathing that the majority society sought to impose, often very effectively.

In the 1960s, most gays needed to remain closeted to avoid blatant hostility and discrimination. A few, however, began to advocate militant actions similar to those of Black Power and other liberation groups. The major problem, especially in urban areas with large gay populations, was outrageous treatment by local law enforcement. In New York and Los Angeles, police officers regularly infiltrated gay bars, beat patrons, and transported them to jail. Small groups of gay activists formed to combat these and other injustices, giving rise to gay and lesbian centers with community outreach programs and newspapers and other information sources.

The dramatic confrontation at the Stonewall Inn, a tavern in New York's Greenwich Village, on June 28, 1969, is generally considered the start of the modern LGBT rights movement. Tired of harassment at the hands of law-enforcement officers, several gay customers at the bar stood their ground and resisted the police. A riot broke out, and other gay men and women soon joined the patrons. Shouts of "gay power" resounded through the establishment. In the next several days, gay demonstrations were held throughout New York City. The Stonewall riots empowered gay people

Larry
Kramer

throughout the country, and gay liberation groups soon formed in most U.S. cities.

The momentum of these groups enabled the gay community to employ the civil rights movement's direct action tactics in response to the AIDS pandemic starting in the 1980s. The key organization was the AIDS Coalition to Unleash Power (ACT UP). Started by playwright Larry Kramer, ACT UP commenced a series of high-profile actions aimed at informing the public of the catastrophic consequences of this disease on the gay community. Demonstrations, occupations, and several mass arrests helped bring the world's attention to the crisis.

In the early 21st century, gay activism has achieved substantial success, despite the continued presence of extensive homophobia across America. After years of protests and lobbying against the "Don't Ask, Don't Tell" policy, gay women and men were allowed to serve openly in the armed forces. A number of states changed their laws to permit same-sex marriage, and in June 2013, the U.S. Supreme Court gave landmark victories to the gay rights movement by invalidating key features of the federal Defense of Marriage Act and by clearing the way for same-sex marriage in California. Especially among younger generations, the LGBT community achieved increasing social acceptance.

All of these groups—Latinos, American Indians, Asian Americans, women, and gays—have followed the footsteps of the civil rights movement in agitating for their own rights and social justice. Others, including members of the disabled community, immigrants, and senior citizens, have likewise used the direct-action strategies and tactics of the civil rights movement to bring attention to their causes and to effect the social changes they desire. Similar agitational enterprises, beyond the realm of civil rights, have also borrowed heavily from the movement. In recent years, animal rights, environmental, anti-globalization, and Occupy Movement activists have made headlines with their dramatic direct actions and civil disobedience protests.

Barack
Obama

AFRICAN AMERICAN CIVIL RIGHTS IN THE EARLY 21ST CENTURY

The African American civil rights movement itself has also continued into the new century. The election of Barack Obama as president of the United States in 2008 suggested to many commentators that America had entered a new, "post-racial" era. Some suggested that the civil rights movement achieved its ultimate victory and that the racism of the past, however destructive and regrettable, should no longer occupy major attention on the nation's public policy agenda.

That view was clearly flawed, concealing—intentionally or not—the pervasive racism that persists at many levels of the American society and economy. The presence of African American officeholders, even at the very highest level, as well as larger numbers of people of color throughout the professional and commercial worlds, reflects real progress, a tribute to the civil rights efforts of the people whose stories are chronicled in this book.

But the economic data speak loudly and depressingly: Into the second decade of the 21st century, the unemployment rate among African Americans remains consistently more than double the rate for white Americans. The figure is especially high for African American youth, exceeding 30 percent for those aged 16–19. And beyond the relentlessly grim numbers, the deplorable conditions facing millions of African Americans in the nation's cities, including poor housing, declining and re-segregated schools, diminishing social services, and a multitude of other problems, are glaringly obvious. Following a 2013 Supreme Court decision that gutted the 1965 Voting Rights Act, several states enacted voter suppression legislation that clearly targeted African American voters. Many, probably most, of these are the inevitable outcome of historical racism and the widespread public indifference among the majority white population itself. This tragic reality reflects the deeper if often unacknowledged racist attitudes that have despoiled American history from the beginning and that have prompted the nation's ongoing civil rights activities

One of the most serious legacies of American racism lies in the criminal justice system. The civil rights movement of the 1950s and 60s rallied around the profound injustices of the Scottsboro boys and the Emmett Till cases, among many others. More recently, civil rights activities have focused on the way people of color, especially younger men, experience racial profiling and unfair treatment in the court system. The 2013 not-guilty verdict for the killer of Trayvon Martin in Florida reminded millions of African Americans, once again, of the way black lives are devalued.

In 2014, several high-profile cases of police killings of blacks triggered protests by the African American community and supporters from other races. In August, an unarmed black teenager was shot by a police officer in Ferguson, Missouri. After a grand jury declined to indict the officer, weeks of street protests followed, in Ferguson and throughout the country. A few weeks earlier, an unarmed black man died after being placed in an illegal chokehold by a New York City policeman in Staten Island, New York. Once again, massive demonstrations occurred following a grand jury decision declining to indict the officer. And in November, a 12-year old boy was shot and killed in Cleveland, Ohio, further intensifying the protests, which continued into 2015. These demonstrations resembled the protests of the 1960s and 1970s in size and intensity. In each case, law enforcement and the justice system faced angry criticism for their failure to respond quickly or fairly against deadly white-on-black violence.

BLACK LIVES MATTER
A MOVEMENT, NOT A MOMENT

BLACK LIVES MATTER is the most recent expression of the civil rights movement.

It began in 2013 after Trayvon Martin's killer was found not guilty. Since then, BLACK LIVES MATTER demonstrations occured throughout the US to protest many black deaths at the hands of the police.

Eric Garner
Killed in Staten island, New York
July 17, 2014

Michael Brown
Killed in Ferguson, Missouri, August 9, 2014

Tamir Rice
Killed in Cleveland Ohio
November 27, 2014

Walter Scott
Killed in North Charleston, South Carolina
April 4, 2015

The contemporary civil rights movement has also demanded change in the rampant racism plaguing the American penal system. Legal scholar Michelle Alexander, in her groundbreaking 2010 book *The New Jim Crow*, revealed the disproportionate population of black men in federal, state, and local prisons and jails. The social consequences of this condition reinforce the historic Jim Crow laws and practices that dominated the national landscape from the nation's inception through much of the 20th century.

Race does still matter in contemporary America. Even as people of color make advances in various fields, a deeper institutional racism persists below the surface. A pernicious feature of that reality is that much of the racism is unconscious, remaining unacknowledged in the media and public discourse. But the long, and now more difficult, battles on the streets and in the courts and in the arena of public opinion must continue. The civil rights movements of the 19th and 20th centuries were merely one phase in a long and complex journey to genuine racial equality and social justice. That campaign will–and should—continue until victory is finally secure.

BIBLIOGRAPHY

The literature on the civil rights movement is enormous. The following books represent a small, highly selective sampling of works that have informed the present volume. Most are available in bookstores, libraries, and online.

Adamson, Madeline, and Seth Borgos. *This Mighty Dream*. Boston: Routledge and Kegan Paul, 1984.

Albert, Judith, and Stewart Albert. *The Sixties Papers*. New York: Praeger, 1984.

Anderson, Jervis. *Bayard Rustin: Troubles I've Seen*. New York: Harper Collins, 1997.

Aptheker, Herbert. *Afro-American History*. New York: Citadel Press, 1971.

Aptheker, Herbert. *American Negro Slave Revolts*. New York: International Publishers, 1970.

Arsenault, Raymond. *The Sound of Freedom: Marian Anderson, The Lincoln Memorial, and the Concert that Awakened America*. New York: Bloomsburg Press, 2009.

Baldwin, James. *The Fire Next Time*. New York: Dell Books, 1964.

Baraka, Amiri. *The Autobiography of LeRoi Jones*. New York: Lawrence Hill Books,

Bass, Patrick H. *Like a Mighty Stream: The March on Washington, August 28, 1963*. Philadelphia: Running Press, 2002.

Bloom, Alexander, and Wini Breines, editors. *Takin' It To The Streets: A Sixties Reader*. New York: Oxford University Press, 1995.

Bloom, Joshua, and Waldo Martin. *Black Against Empire: The History and Politics of the Black Panther Party*. Berkeley: University of California Press, 2013.

Bond, Julian, and Anthony Lewis, editors. *Gonna Sit at the Welcome Table*. New York: American Heritage/Forbes, 1995.

Boyd, Herb. *We Shall Overcome*. Naperville, Illinois: Sourcebooks, C2004.

Braden, Anne. *The Wall Between*. New York: Marzini and Munsell, 1959.

Branch, Taylor. *At Canaan's Edge: America in the King Years, 1965-68*. New York: Simon and Schuster, 2006.

Branch, Taylor. *Parting the Waters: America in the King Years, 1954-63*. New York: Simon and Schuster, 1988.

Branch, Taylor. *Pillars of Fire: America in the King Years, 1963-65*. New York: Simon and Schuster, 1998.

Brown, Elaine. *A Taste of Power*. New York: Pantheon Books, 1997.

Brown, Scot. *Fighting for US*. New York: New York University Press, 2003.

Cagin, Seth, and Philip Dray. *We Are Not Afraid: The Story of Goodman, Schwerner, and Cheney and the Civil Rights Campaign for Mississippi*. New York: Nation Books, 2006.

Carmichael, Stokely, and Charles Hamilton. *Black Power: The Politics of Liberation in America*. New York: Random House, 1967.

Carmichael, Stokely. *Stokely Speaks: Black Power Back to Pan-Africanism*. New York: Vintage Books, 1967.

Carson, Claybourne et al., eds. *The Eyes on the Prize Civil Rights Reader*. New York: Penguin, 1991.

Carson, Claybourne. *In Struggle: SNCC and the Black Awakening of the 1960s*. Cambridge: Harvard University Press, 1981.

Cashman, Sean D. *African-Americans and the Quest for Civil Rights, 1900-1990*. New York: New York University Press, 1991.

Cobb, Charles E. *This Nonviolent Stuff'll Get You Killed*. New York: Basic Books, 2014.

Douglass, Frederick. *Narrative of the Life of Frederick Douglass*. New York: Dover Publishers, 1995.

Durant, Sam. *Black Panther: The Revolutionary Art of Emory Douglas*. New York: Rizzoli International Publishers, 2007.

Dyson, Michael Eric. *Making Malcolm: The Myth and Meaning of Malcolm X*. New York: Oxford University Press, 1995.

Etheridge, Eric. *Breach of Peach: Portraits of the 1961 Mississippi Freedom Riders*. New York: Atlas and Co., 2008.

Garrow, David. *Bearing the Cross: Martin Luther King Jr. and the Southern Christian Leadership Conference*. New York: Harper, 1999.

Haley, Alex. *The Autobiography of Malcolm X*. New York: Ballantine Books, 1998.

Hamilton, Charles V. *Adam Clayton Powell, Jr*. New York: Collier Books, 1991.

Harding, Vincent. *There is a River: The Black Struggle for Freedom in America*. New York: Harcourt Brace Jovanovich, 1981.

Harris, William H. *Keeping the Faith: A. Philip Randolph, Milton Webster, and the Brotherhood of Sleeping Car Porters, 1925-37*. Urbana, Illinois: University of Illinois Press, 1991.

Horne, Gerald. *The Fire This Time: The Watts Uprising and the 1960s*. Charlottesville: University of Virginia Press, 1995.

Jackson, Esther Cooper, ed. *Freedomways Reader*. Boulder, Colorado: Westview Press, 2000.

Joseph, Peniel. *Stokely: A Life*. New York: Basic/Civitas, 2014.

Joseph, Peniel, ed. *The Black Power Movement: Rethinking the Civil Right-Black Power Era*. New York: Routledge, 2006.

Joseph, Peniel. *Waiting 'Til The Midnight Hour: A Narrative History of Black Power in America*. New York: Henry Holt, 2006.

Lemelle, Sid. *Pan-Africanism For Beginners*. New York: Writers and Readers, 1992.

Lewis, David Levering. *W.E.B. DuBois: The Fight for Equality and the American Century, 1916-1963*. New York: Henry Holt, 2000.

Marable, Manning. *Malcolm X: A Life of Reinvention*. New York: Penguin, 2011.

Mills, Kay. *This Little Light of Mine: The Life of Fannie Lou Hamer*. New York: Dutton, 1993.

Moody, Anne. *Coming of Age in Mississippi*. New York: Dial Press, 1968.

Morgan, Robin, editor. *Sisterhood is Powerful*. New York: Vintage books, 1970.

Raines, Howell, ed. *My Soul is Rested: The Story of the Civil Rights Movement in the Deep South*. New York: Penguin, 1983.

Robeson, Paul. *Here I Stand*. Boston: Beacon Press, 1988.

Segrue, Thomas. *Sweet Land of Liberty: The Forgotten Struggle for Civil Rights in the North*. New York: Random House, 2008.

Von Blum, Paul. *Racism and the Law*. San Diego: Cognella, 2012.

Williams, Robert F. *Negroes With Guns*. New York: Marzani and Munsell, 1962.

Young, Ralph, ed. *Dissent in America*. New York: Pearson Longman, 2008.

Zinn, Howard. *SNCC, The New Abolitionists*. Boston: Beacon Press, 1964.

ABOUT THE AUTHOR
AND ILLUSTRATOR

PAUL VON BLUM is Senior Lecturer in African American Studies and Communication Studies at UCLA. He is the author of six books and numerous articles on art, culture, education, and politics. His most recent book is *A Life at the Margins: Keeping the Political Vision*, his 2011 memoir that chronicles almost 50 years of political activism, starting with his civil rights work in the South and elsewhere in the early 1960s. Paul lives in Los Angeles, CA.

FRANK REYNOSO is a Brooklyn-based writer, cartoonist, and illustrator. His comics have appeared in *BRKLYNR*, *Mint*, *World War 3 Illustrated*, and *Occupy Comics*. And he's done illustrations for *The Physics of the Impossible* on the Science channel, and Mayfair Games. He enjoys horror, science fiction, and comedy with a glass of wine.

THE FOR BEGINNERS® SERIES

AFRICAN HISTORY FOR BEGINNERS: ISBN 978-1-934389-18-8
ANARCHISM FOR BEGINNERS: ISBN 978-1-934389-32-4
ARABS & ISRAEL FOR BEGINNERS: ISBN 978-1-934389-16-4
ART THEORY FOR BEGINNERS: ISBN 978-1-934389-47-8
ASTRONOMY FOR BEGINNERS: ISBN 978-1-934389-25-6
AYN RAND FOR BEGINNERS: ISBN 978-1-934389-37-9
BARACK OBAMA FOR BEGINNERS, AN ESSENTIAL GUIDE: ISBN 978-1-934389-44-7
BEN FRANKLIN FOR BEGINNERS: ISBN 978-1-934389-48-5
BLACK HISTORY FOR BEGINNERS: ISBN 978-1-934389-19-5
THE BLACK HOLOCAUST FOR BEGINNERS: ISBN 978-1-934389-03-4
BLACK PANTHERS FOR BEGINNERS: ISBN 978-1-939994-39-4
BLACK WOMEN FOR BEGINNERS: ISBN 978-1-934389-20-1
BUDDHA FOR BEGINNERS   ISBN 978-1-939994-33-2
BUKOWSKI FOR BEGINNERS   ISBN 978-1-939994-37-0
CHOMSKY FOR BEGINNERS: ISBN 978-1-934389-17-1
DADA & SURREALISM FOR BEGINNERS: ISBN 978-1-934389-00-3
DANTE FOR BEGINNERS: ISBN 978-1-934389-67-6
DECONSTRUCTION FOR BEGINNERS: ISBN 978-1-934389-26-3
DEMOCRACY FOR BEGINNERS: ISBN 978-1-934389-36-2
DERRIDA FOR BEGINNERS: ISBN 978-1-934389-11-9
EASTERN PHILOSOPHY FOR BEGINNERS: ISBN 978-1-934389-07-2
EXISTENTIALISM FOR BEGINNERS: ISBN 978-1-934389-21-8
FANON FOR BEGINNERS   ISBN 978-1-934389-87-4
FDR AND THE NEW DEAL FOR BEGINNERS: ISBN 978-1-934389-50-8
FOUCAULT FOR BEGINNERS: ISBN 978-1-934389-12-6
FRENCH REVOLUTIONS FOR BEGINNERS: ISBN 978-1-934389-91-1
GENDER & SEXUALITY FOR BEGINNERS: ISBN 978-1-934389-69-0
GLOBAL WARMING FOR BEGINNERS: ISBN 978-1-934389-27-0
GREEK MYTHOLOGY FOR BEGINNERS: ISBN 978-1-934389-83-6
HEIDEGGER FOR BEGINNERS: ISBN 978-1-934389-13-3
THE HISTORY OF CLASSICAL MUSIC FOR BEGINNERS: ISBN 978-1-939994-26-4
THE HISTORY OF OPERA FOR BEGINNERS: ISBN 978-1-934389-79-9
ISLAM FOR BEGINNERS: ISBN 978-1-934389-01-0
JANE AUSTEN FOR BEGINNERS: ISBN 978-1-934389-61-4
JUNG FOR BEGINNERS: ISBN 978-1-934389-76-8
KIERKEGAARD FOR BEGINNERS: ISBN 978-1-934389-14-0
LACAN FOR BEGINNERS: ISBN 978-1-934389-39-3
LINCOLN FOR BEGINNERS: ISBN 978-1-934389-85-0
LINGUISTICS FOR BEGINNERS: ISBN 978-1-934389-28-7
MALCOLM X FOR BEGINNERS: ISBN 978-1-934389-04-1
MARX'S *DAS KAPITAL* FOR BEGINNERS: ISBN 978-1-934389-59-1
MCLUHAN FOR BEGINNERS: ISBN 978-1-934389-75-1
MUSIC THEORY FOR BEGINNERS: ISBN 978-1-939994-46-2
NIETZSCHE FOR BEGINNERS: ISBN 978-1-934389-05-8
PAUL ROBESON FOR BEGINNERS   ISBN 978-1-934389-81-2
PHILOSOPHY FOR BEGINNERS: ISBN 978-1-934389-02-7
PLATO FOR BEGINNERS: ISBN 978-1-934389-08-9
POETRY FOR BEGINNERS: ISBN 978-1-934389-46-1
POSTMODERNISM FOR BEGINNERS: ISBN 978-1-934389-09-6
RELATIVITY & QUANTUM PHYSICS FOR BEGINNERS: ISBN 978-1-934389-42-3
SARTRE FOR BEGINNERS: ISBN 978-1-934389-15-7
SAUSSURE FOR BEGINNERS   ISBN 978-1-939994-41-7
SHAKESPEARE FOR BEGINNERS: ISBN 978-1-934389-29-4
STANISLAVSKI FOR BEGINNERS   ISBN 978-1-939994-35-6
STRUCTURALISM & POSTSTRUCTURALISM FOR BEGINNERS: ISBN 978-1-934389-10-2
WOMEN'S HISTORY FOR BEGINNERS: ISBN 978-1-934389-60-7
UNIONS FOR BEGINNERS: ISBN 978-1-934389-77-5
U.S. CONSTITUTION FOR BEGINNERS: ISBN 978-1-934389-62-1
ZEN FOR BEGINNERS: ISBN 978-1-934389-06-5
ZINN FOR BEGINNERS: ISBN 978-1-934389-40-9

www.forbeginnersbooks.com